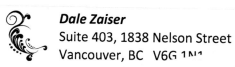

From Rage to Resolution

From Rage

To Resolution

By
DeAnne Rosenberg

iUniverse, Inc.
New York   Bloomington

From Rage to Resolution
Conquering Conflict

iUniverse books may be ordered through booksellers or by contacting:

iUniverse
1663 Liberty Drive
Bloomington, IN 47403
www.iuniverse.com
1-800-Authors (1-800-288-4677)

ISBN: 978-1-4502-6169-2 (sc)
ISBN: 978-1-4502-6170-8 (dj)
ISBN: 978-1-4502-6306-1 (ebk)

Library of Congress Control Number: 2010914497

Printed in the United States of America

iUniverse rev. date: 10/21/2010

Dedication

To my sister, Gail Ludvigson, whose intelligence, positive spirit, bravery, and determination in the face of monumental challenges will be a continuing inspiration to all who knew and loved her.

To Carl Kalithasan Sevasamy, who proves every day that with knowledge, wisdom, and patience, abundance is possible.

Acknowledgments

My grateful thanks to my superb computer wiz and illustrator, Myron Lewis for his inspiring guidance and constant source of good ideas. His guidance helped me to create something truly worthwhile. My thanks also to Lee Tapp, my best friend forever, for her assistance with the organization and editing. I could not have done this work without her advocacy and enthusiasm for the project. Since every single story in this book is true, I also wish to gratefully thank all those wonderful people who shared their private pain with me. I hope my advice made a difference. Last but by no means least, my thanks to the wonderful staff at iUniverse without whose thoughtful critique, encouragement, and suggestions this work would never have been completed.

Contents

Preface

A CHILD'S EXPRESSION OF RAGE and anger is so pure and unadulterated by layers of so-called civilized acceptable behavior that it is easy to read. Take, for example, the following story.

Six-year-old Miles is on the left side of the front porch, building a construction site with Legos. His eighteen-month-old sister, Angela, is ensconced in her playpen, happily whacking away at an aluminum pot with a wooden cooking spoon. Their mother, Lynne, although busy with housework, checks up on her children every few minutes.

Earlier that morning, Lynne had placed a number of unwanted items of furniture and boxes of clothing at the curb to be picked up by Goodwill Industries later that day. This time when she looks out to see what her children are doing, she sees that Miles has taken Angela out of her playpen and put her, along with the pot and wooden spoon, right on top of the items slated for Goodwill.

With adults, the acting out of rage is more subtle, which means that getting to the real problem can be a more difficult challenge. Here is an example.

A high-tech company employs scientists of various disciplines, with multiple degrees in very esoteric areas of science, to keep them ahead of their competitors. Recruiting, interviewing, and hiring such people is the central mission of the company's personnel manager, Alice Jason. Alice is also responsible for health insurance records, salary studies, safety issues, government reports, as well as the recruitment of scientists.

Alice has not taken the time to learn the details of what occupies the company's scientific staff. When she locates a viable candidate—a scientist with the appropriate background, experience, and education—she asks one of the staff scientists to assist her in the interviewing process. Alice handles the basic areas of the interview and leaves the technical and scientific questions to the scientist.

During a six-month period, none of these very valuable candidates accepted an offer of employment. The company president was extremely troubled over the situation and asked Alice to find out why. Alice discovered that all the candidates felt they had been rudely treated and often insulted by the scientific staff member who had interviewed them. Alice concluded that the scientists needed a training session in interviewing techniques. She engaged a training consultant to present the workshop.

What often happens in the consulting business is the problem identified by the company is not the issue at all, but rather a symptom of something else. In my thirty-five years of doing this kind of work, I've seen that most problems were the result of somebody retaliating against a situation that enraged and angered them. In this particular situation, the consultant found, upon speaking with the members of the scientific staff, that there was a great deal of rage toward Alice.

> "We work on very difficult technical problems requiring long hours of intense concentration and many time-sensitive, complicated tests. This dumb broad (Alice) interrupts us to do interviews. That's her job, not ours. In her three years at this place, she has never bothered to learn what we do. She still doesn't understand the science or the terminology. She has no respect for our time. She just demands we drop everything to do her job for her."

The consultant told Alice that her scientists did not need an interviewing skills workshop. Their hostile behavior toward the candidates was actually a result of their rage at being interrupted in their work to assist her with her responsibility. Alice was not receptive to hearing the truth. She became hostile and expressed her anger by immediately terminating the consultant. (Kill the messenger!)

It seemed to me that a book which takes examples of ambiguous hostile reactions from both home and work might just help a person recognize how rage bubbles up in daily life. Teaching people how to recognize this behavior and showing them how to deal with it might be a valuable skill. This is part of what you will learn from reading this book.

Understanding the psychology or the theory behind rage might be interesting, but it is not very useful. After all, most of us do not deal with mentally ill people. We deal with normal folks who are attempting to express their righteous hostility in socially acceptable ways. Sometimes, through no fault of our own, we get caught up in that web of rage. Because we do not recognize it for what it is, we can find no way to deal with it, except to retaliate with our own rage. This reaction, although thoroughly understandable, only escalates the situation. Part of the problem is that rage appears in various disguises. Here are a few examples:

Rage can be a mask for low self-esteem or can be used to conceal personal failures. Sometimes anger toward others is merely a projection of the rage a person feels toward him- or herself because of unmet expectations. When those expectations suddenly come to light, rage is generated. This is what happened between Alice and the consultant.

Rage can hide vulnerability. Rage can be a demand that one's boundaries be respected or one's importance be acknowledged and recognized. Both these demands result from feelings of vulnerability. This was the reason behind the reaction of the scientists who were asked to conduct interviews.

Angry accusations can be a confession. Sometimes people who feel guilty about something they have done will furiously accuse someone else of having done it. This strategy diverts attention away from them.

Angry insults can conceal jealousy. An insult says more about the speaker than it does about the target of the remark. The insult may actually disclose the speaker's jealousy regarding a character strength which the other person possesses.

Rage can look like compliant passivity. Public compliance often hides private rage. Passivity does not mean agreement. It is an aggressive act using inertia and mistakes to block someone else's action. A person can also assume a *loser role* to disguise an attempt at gaining power over others.

Rage and defensiveness can screen egoism. Sometimes people become enraged and defensive because they mistakenly assume that a disagreement is directed at them personally. Such people are unable to separate their ideas from their identity. If you have ever tried to discuss a point with a religious or political zealot, you have experienced this reaction.

Rage can masquerade as withdrawal. Sometimes extremely angry people will withdraw from conflict, in order to avoid what they know would be uncontrollable rage if they let it loose. Withdrawal is their only safe alternative. This is the *nice, quiet* boy who, in rage, guns down his classmates.

Throughout this book, you will see actual examples of these manifestations of rage and anger. You will become an expert at recognizing when other people act out of their hostilities. Best of all, you will know exactly how to respond without becoming emotionally entangled in their rage. You will see how others use anger as a tool in many common situations:

- When they feel their personal space has been invaded and they feel violated

- When they feel their needs are not being met or recognized
- When they have been treated disrespectfully
- When they want to force people into confronting a current situation
- When they want to manipulate another person so they get their own way

You will understand the unfortunate truth that when a person uses rage and anger, it is really impossible for them to clearly and honestly communicate their issues in words others can hear. Others recognize the rage but fail to take in the actual message of the words. This forces the angry person to seek third-party intervention in the person of lawyers, union stewards, and EEO personnel.

Here is an illustration of this last point. Jim and Pete were assigned to work together on a project and to split the workload equally. Jim is a smoker; Pete is not. Jim takes a twenty-minute smoking break once every hour. This results in Pete doing most of the work. Pete has asked Jim to limit his smoking to the legitimate lunch and coffee breaks. Jim explains he cannot do that, because he is addicted to cigarettes. Furious, Pete angrily demands his boss resolve the problem. The boss reacts badly to Pete's rage and tells him to solve the problem himself. In frustration, Pete files a discrimination complaint.

Those in the personnel department recognize that Pete's discrimination complaint is not a valid legal issue, but they do not know how to make this legal challenge go away. Personnel's solution is to pay Pete a monetary *nuisance award*. The organization continues the practice of paying off these bogus discrimination complaints, until the total of nuisance awards reaches one hundred thousand dollars. At that point, a consultant is called in to find a way for the employees to resolve their frustrations without seeking a legal remedy.

The consultant's solution is to teach both managers and employees the skills of conflict resolution. This is what you will learn from this book: how to resolve your rage issues by using a well-defined series of conversational steps and strategies. Never again will you have to exhibit rage behaviors to get your problems resolved. Never again will you be victimized by your own rage or by the rage behavior of others. Such behavior can permanently damage a marriage or career and scar children for life. Rage behavior, although righteous, shows others a level of emotional immaturity and behavioral unpredictability. In addition, it invites reprisal from those subjected to it.

DeAnne Rosenberg
Widow's Cove
2010

Do I Need to Read This Book Inventory

Instructions: Using a scale of 1–10, please score yourself on the following statements in the space provided.

1	5	10
Yes; true	Sometimes, maybe	No; never

1. I know that depression is an anger reaction turned inward against myself. _____

2. I am able to read other people's body language and respond appropriately. _____

3. If I am faced with extreme hostility, I know how to react so that I remain safe. _____

4. If someone is disturbing me by talking aloud in a movie or concert, I have no problem asking them to be quiet. _____

5. If someone is smoking near me, and the smoke is bothering me, I would not move to another area. _____

6. If someone or something gets me very, very angry
   (rage), I am able to unload my hostility by engaging in
   strenuous physical activities.   _____

7. I have the skills to negotiate any problem or conflict to a
   win-win outcome.   _____

8. If a good friend makes an unreasonable request, I can
   easily refuse him or her.   _____

9. Should my boss make an unreasonable request, I refuse
   to accommodate him or her   _____

10. Unwarranted criticism does not make me angry or
    depressed, because I know how to respond to it.   _____

11. I know five methods for managing my own anger.   _____

12. I know three strategies for making sure the rage of others
    does not affect me.   _____

13. I do not resort to clever ways of getting even with people
    who I think have done me wrong.   _____

14. I never try to bottle up my anger; I'd rather risk making
    a scene.   _____

15. I do not allow other people to exploit or push me around. _____

16. I can spot passive-aggressive behavior, and I understand
    how to deal with it.   _____

17. I recognize the types of situations in which the five traditional methods of conflict resolution work best. _____

18. I can identify the many forms of manipulative criticism, and I know how to respond to each one of them effectively. _____

19. I am comfortable stating my views to authority figures (boss, doctor, etc.). _____

20. When someone or something makes me very, very angry (rage), I am careful not to take my rage out on my spouse or children. _____

21. I can confront a person who is annoying me without insulting them. _____

22. I can defend my views to a group of people who do not agree with me. _____

23. If someone interrupts me, I speak up immediately. _____

24. I tell my spouse and children when I think they are taking advantage of me. _____

25. When someone criticizes me, I discuss their comments frankly with them. _____

26. I invite criticism from my boss about my work. _____

27. I refuse to apologize, even when expected to, if I feel I am right. _____

28. I have five different strategies for resolving conflicts. _____

29. I understand how to expose the origin of a conflict. _____

30. I can discriminate between situations that require collaboration from those that need compromise. _____

31. I can give a staff member a negative performance appraisal with no problem. _____

32. I turn down requests for visits and favors because I simply don't feel like it. _____

33. I tell my boss when I believe he or she is wrong. _____

34. If I believe a person is trying to manipulate me, I call them on it. _____

35. I speak up immediately when I think a person is patronizing me. _____

36. I express my anger immediately when I experience it. _____

37. I know exactly how to prepare for a successful verbal confrontation. _____

38. If someone is discourteous or rude to me, I speak up immediately. _____

39. If I have staff members in conflict, I know how to help mediate a resolution. _____

40. If I think I have been overcharged for a product or service, I confront the person immediately and get the matter resolved. _____

41. I understand that showing fear to a person who is aggressive and hostile only encourages them to escalate their rage. _____

42. I have the tools to decelerate a hostile situation. _____

43. I know five methods for resolving conflict within a work team. _____

44. I recognize that public compliance often hides private rage. _____

45. I am very much aware that my taking a hardnosed stance on anything can result in a desire for reprisal from the other person. _____

Scoring the Results:

Add up your scores for all forty-five items. The higher your score, the more help this book will be in restoring you to full control of your life.

50	250	500
You are in full control of your life.	Anger is still getting the best of you.	You really need this book

Chapter One

～

Introduction

CONVENTIONAL WISDOM SUGGESTS THAT CONFLICT is a bad thing. People who find themselves in a conflict situation, therefore, must be inept at managing their lives. If that were true, it would mean that everyone must be inept at managing their lives, because conflict is an inherent part of living and being human.

There is nothing simple about conflict. It is convoluted, complex, confusing, and untidy, in that it embodies three problems:

- the issue itself
- how to address the issue
- to whom you should speak regarding the issue

Take, for example, the following situation. Your spouse pressures you to lend her brother ten thousand dollars. Although you believe that the brother is irresponsible and reckless, especially where other people's money is concerned, you agree to make the loan in order to avoid a conflict with your spouse.

Six months pass, and the brother has not paid back one cent. You are upset with yourself, because you knew better than to make the loan. You are angry with your spouse for putting pressure on you to make the loan in the first place. And you are furious with the irresponsible brother, who has made no attempt at repayment of the loan. You discuss the issue with your spouse, who asks that you not say anything to the brother right now, because, "He's under a lot of stress." With that statement, *your* stress increases tenfold.

Your spouse and the deadbeat brother are close. Often your families get together for a night out. The brother phones and says, "Why don't we get together this weekend? Maybe we could take in a movie or go out to dinner." When you hear his voice, you start to seethe. Your teeth begin to grind. You can't help yourself, as you respond, "We can't afford to go out to dinner, because we've lent money to people *who won't pay us back—a-hem!*"

The brother isn't stupid. He gets your message. He then launches into a litany of reasons why he hasn't been able to repay the loan. "You know I'd have paid you back if I could, but Judy needed orthodontics, Jerry's tuition was due, Jeanie had her appendix out, and Joey needed help with his auto insurance." Obviously you now have more information than you want. Moreover, you feel like a heel for even mentioning the loan.

On the other hand, after your comment explaining why you cannot go out to dinner, he might respond: "Why do you need the money back? What are you going to do with it, anyway?" And you tell him: "Mary needs orthodontics, Matt's tuition is due, Maddie has to have her appendix out, and Martin needs help with his auto insurance."

Now he has more information than *he* wants. Moreover, he might even argue with you about how you are planning to spend the money.

"I'm sure the dentist will wait for his money; I thought you told me that Matt was on scholarship; your medical insurance policy should take care of Maddie's medical bills; and Martin is working full time, so he ought to be handling his own auto expenses."

Or, suppose the brother becomes extremely angry when you hint about the overdue loan and yells at you, "My God! What's the big deal? Do you think I'm going to screw you out of a lousy ten thousand dollars?" How should you respond? Should you get equally angry, or should you back off?

In the end, no matter how the conversation goes, not only do you not have the money back, your friendship with the brother and his family is forever damaged. Most importantly, you are now carrying a heavy load of unresolved anger toward your spouse. In addition, you feel depressed and infuriated with yourself. You have proven that you are the world's biggest moron. Your inner voice tells you, "Undoubtedly you deserve to lose the money."

As this situation illustrates, the existence of conflict creates enormous amounts of anxiety and self-loathing (and sometimes fear) in a number of directions, for several reasons:

- You worry that saying anything might make the situation worse.
- You brood about a possible loss of emotional control—yours as well as the other person's.
- You agonize that the long-term effects will generate a desire for reprisal on the part of the other person.
- You despair that efforts at conflict resolution will be a win-lose exercise and that you are likely to end up on the losing end.

Suppose you decide that it is best to say nothing at all about the loan and hope that your brother-in-law will eventually pay back the money. As the months go by with no mention or repayment of the loan, you begin to fantasize about interesting ways of torturing your brother-in-law:

- By ordering Chinese takeout deliveries from sixteen different establishments, all to arrive at his home at the same time
- By infesting his home with hundreds of mice or other noxious four-legged creatures

- By telephoning him at home at 2:00 AM and 3:00 AM every night and, when he answers, saying, "Sorry, wrong number."
- By hiring a *Sopranos* henchman to break his kneecaps

Of course, the longer this situation goes on, the more malevolent your fantasies become. Now when your families get together, you sit silently making faces at your brother-in-law. When he asks you what's the matter, through gritted teeth, you respond with a curt "Nothing!"

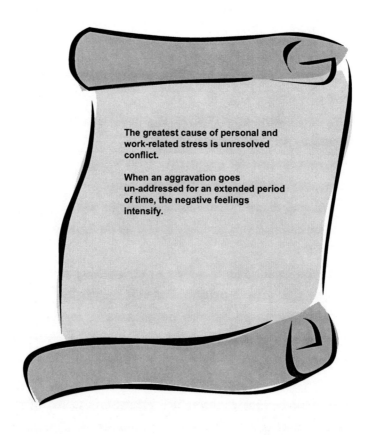

The greatest cause of personal and work-related stress is unresolved conflict.

When an aggravation goes un-addressed for an extended period of time, the negative feelings intensify.

The brother-in-law is now uncomfortable in your presence, and so your families meet less often. You think this is probably a good thing, because he won't have the opportunity to pressure your spouse into asking you for yet another loan. Your ultimate surprise comes when, months later, you receive a postcard from Argentina. He tells you he has moved the family to the Patagonian region, where they are going to raise lamas.

A work situation can generate the same kind of frustration and hostility. Kevin was hired by a very prestigious banking firm. He was a fast learner with a pleasant personality and so was quickly promoted. He was assigned to work closely with the senior vice president. Unfortunately, the senior vice president had a problem with Kevin's name and kept calling him Kermit.

Early on, Kevin thought about correcting his boss but decided that was probably unwise. He wanted their relationship to work smoothly and believed that telling the boss he was wrong was not in his best interest. As the months went by, the Kermit epithet began to really annoy Kevin. Not only did the Kermit name generate a good deal of ribbing from his co-workers and customers, those outside his immediate work area began to call him Kermit, as well. Soon, each time someone called him Kermit his stress level would spike, and he would grind his teeth. Co-workers began to wonder what ever happened to Kevin's congenial attitude and cooperative demeanor, because he seemed out-of-sorts most of the time.

Kevin realized he was in trouble. When he went to Personnel to discuss the issue, the counselor told him: "If the old man has been calling you Kermit for the last five months, it's a little late in the game for you to correct him now. It would only embarrass him and make him angry. You know how negatively rigid he is about mistakes. He will ask you why you didn't say anything about this before. What can you say? My best advice to you is that you live with it. The old man is due to retire in eighteen months. I'm certain you can hang in there for that amount of time."

Kevin made a valiant effort to ignore his boss's calling him Kermit. His discomfort, however, showed. The boss could see the tension in Kevin's body and hear the stress in Kevin's voice every time they talked. Eventually, his boss interpreted Kevin's negative reactions to mean that he was unhappy with the job or with his boss. Six months after being hired, Kevin was told to seek employment elsewhere.

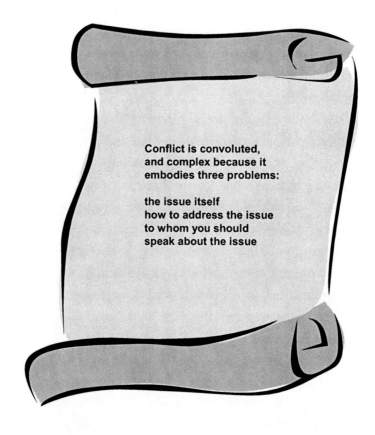

Conflict is convoluted,
and complex because it
embodies three problems:

the issue itself
how to address the issue
to whom you should
speak about the issue

Why is it so difficult for people to give voice to their very legitimate anger? Are we fearful that whatever we say will create more difficulties than we will solve? Are we scared that things might get out of control if we are thought to be offensive for speaking up? Are we troubled that we do not have tools appropriate for confronting another person?

Perhaps we should arm ourselves so that we are fully prepared to handle our own rage and the rage of others. This book is designed to help us meet and conquer the irritating issues that plague our daily lives.

Chapter Two

Looking at the History of the Problem

PEOPLE BEHAVE PRETTY MUCH WITHIN certain norms, whether at home, school, work, the mall, in traffic, or wherever. Those whose behavior is recognized to be far outside those norms are already in institutions or prisons or hopefully headed there.

Stress and conflict are staples in our lives. They are ubiquitous. When stress and conflict besiege us, it feels as though we are being driven outside those normal boundaries of behavior. Deep down, our fear is that we will succumb and act out inappropriately. Therefore, we attempt to imprison our distress internally. No one is fooled, however. We all recognize one another's stress anyway. Perhaps that is why our century has been termed *The Age of Anxiety*. The more economically and technically advanced our society becomes, the more pressure is put on us. As we become more and more anxiety-ridden; we also become less prepared to cope with stress and conflict in nonviolent ways.

Every day there is a new instance of someone shooting and killing others. We hear of it going on in homes against family members, at schools against fellow students, in workplaces against co-workers, at malls against strangers, and on street corners in random drive-by shootings. We ask ourselves, "What is going on in this society? Are we degenerating into a mass of uncivilized and deranged creatures?"

What we are seeing today are the results of generations of us being taught to grit our teeth and bear it. The truth, however, is that experiencing anger and hostility is as much a part of being human as is experiencing joy and love.

As youngsters, we were taught that experiencing and expressing anger was not a good thing and that to act out our hostility was appalling. We have been indoctrinated to believe that a civilized person never exhibits this troublesome emotion.

The hostility we see in our world is a product of the stress and anxiety most of us experience on a daily basis. We simply get overloaded, and, much like a pressure cooker, we explode. Consider how most of us start our days—we listen to the news. Is there ever anything on the news that is *not* stressful? Try counting the number of items the news report offers you, on any given day, that add to your worries:

- Global warming
- Taxes
- Traffic accidents and tie-ups
- Higher prices for food and energy
- Terrorism

If you survive the news, there's the drive to work. Here, utter strangers threaten your existence by manipulating their vehicles with one hand while drinking coffee with the other, and, of course, talking on their cell phones at the same time.

Once you get to work, you learn that the project you expected to be completed and on your desk will be delayed several days. There is an e-mail from your boss informing you that, because of economic conditions, there will be no raises this year. The boss then asks you to select one person from your team to be let go, as another cost-saving measure. The e-mail closes with an apology for adding to your frustrations, but he/she is certain you understand, because you are a team player.

Please notice that all the anger-generating situations described here are things over which you have little control. You did not personally create these situations, and you have no useful tools for changing any of them in a way that would create a positive outcome for you.

Human beings have a very limited capacity for holding aggravation inside.

At some point we need a way to unload our distress.

Without unloading, we are in danger of exploding.

Human beings do not have an unlimited capacity for holding stress and aggravation inside. At some point, we need a way to unload some of that hostility. Grinding our teeth and holding everything inside just doesn't do it for most of us. Some of us use sports and exercise to lower our stress levels; others take to drinking; some use prayer; and still others take out their exasperation on others, by using loud and angry outbursts or abusing their animals. Eventually, most of us find some socially acceptable method for unloading the hostility generated by frustrating circumstances that affect us personally and over which we have little influence.

It is easy to become paranoid, to believe that others are out to *get us*. We know that really isn't true—but it certainly feels that way. Why? It is because we don't actually control many aspects of our lives. In many situations, we are just pawns in someone else's chess game.

What about youngsters and those whose behavior cannot be considered adult? These are individuals who do not have coping methods for dealing with their hostility. For most kids, childhood is a nightmare. Survival and happiness depend upon those over whom one has no power. Think about your own experience as a youngster.

- Were you in the in-crowd, or were you an outsider?
- Were you teased because you wore glasses?
- Were you ridiculed because you were overweight?
- Were you always the last person chosen for the kick-ball or baseball team?
- Did you skip the prom because you could not get a date?
- Were you ostracized because you were a lot smarter than the others?
- Were your parents financially unable to dress you in the accepted *mode du jour*?
- If you were bullied, did you have the skills to respond appropriately?
- Were you ever compared to others in your group who were smarter or better looking than you and asked why you could not be more like them?
- Did you suffer from embarrassing acne?
- Were you heckled because you refused to smoke pot and/ or drink?

- Were you goaded into doing things you knew were wrong just to be an accepted member of some clique?

If we consider the lack of coping skills most children have for dealing with their anger and frustrations, we begin to understand why some youngsters literally go berserk. In the aftermath of the all-too-frequent situations in which youngsters bring guns to school and kill their classmates, it is enlightening to examine the writings they leave behind. Their words attempt to justify their acting out because of an overwhelming frustration. Similar word patterns occur again and again in these situations, not only at school, but in the workplace and in the home—wherever these heinous actions occur. Phrases include

get even
showed all of you
no other choice
you forced me to
trapped
no other way out
couldn't let them get away with that
couldn't take it any more

From the comments listed above, we begin to see the common sources of violent hostility:

- The person is on psychic modifiers such as alcohol or drugs.
- The person believes he/she is under attack and/or in great danger.
- The person is under extreme pressure from some set of circumstances.
- The person feels cornered and sees no way out of his/her predicament.

- The person is extremely angry and has no skills in anger management.
- The person is reacting to the frustration of unmet, maybe even unspoken, expectations.
- The person believes he/she has been taken advantage of one too many times.

The most potent of these is the hostility created as the result of unmet, maybe even unspoken expectations.

As an example, consider the teenager who asks his parents for permission to attend a neighborhood party where liquor will be served and there will be no adult supervision. The parent says, "Absolutely not!" The teenager slams the door to his room in anger and, later on, climbs out a window to attend the party, anyway. Much later, at the police station, the parent asks the child, "Why did you sneak out to this party after I said you could not go?" The teenager responds, "Everyone else's parents allowed their kids to go. But you're so old-fashioned you never let me have any fun. I was not going to let you get away with treating me that way again, so I went to the party, anyway."

In our search for reasons for this escalating violence, we point fingers at lax gun control laws and at television. Those are easy targets. The problem is much more complicated than that. Perhaps we should examine the conventional practice in our society whereby children are brought up to believe that the emotion known as *anger* is a bad thing. That is as ridiculous as saying sorrow is a bad thing. People cannot help how they may feel. They can only make decisions about what they are going to do about how they feel.

To illustrate this point, let's suppose you are at the funeral of a loved one. You are crying and clearly showing that you are quite grief-stricken. A well-meaning friend says, "You shouldn't be sad. She lived a full and rewarding life." You realize your friend is only trying to be helpful, but his words strike you as shallow and insensitive. Wouldn't it be so much better if the friend had said, "She was a wonderful person and I know you will miss her a great deal. Just know that I am here for you." The second comment legitimizes your sorrow and allows you the freedom to demonstrate your grief publicly.

Now let's suppose that your child is very angry about some incident that happened at school and says, "I'm gonna go back tomorrow and punch Johnny right in the chops."

The typical parental response might be, "Now, listen here. You will not punch anyone. In the first place, that's not right. Nice people don't do things like that. And, in the second place, violence solves nothing. It only makes the other person angry."

Instead, the parent should try legitimizing the child's anger. Allow him the freedom to express and experience his feelings. Ask him what happened and listen to his tale of woe. When the parent has a pretty good picture of what happened, she can say: "No wonder you're so angry. If that happened to me, I'd be angry too. So, since you'll be seeing Johnny tomorrow, let's talk about how you want to handle that situation. What do you think you want to say to him about what happened today?" What this parent has done is:

- show the child that he is totally in control of his anger;
- make it very clear that it is completely okay to be angry; and
- that the child should plan some action to defuse that anger by confronting the situation that generated it.

Recognizing that acting out is a product of holding anger inside, many parents have found it helpful to hang a few punching bags in their garage. One might have a female wig on it, the other a moustache and man's wig. When the children are angry, they can be encouraged to go to the garage and have it out—with the punching bag as the offending party.

We cannot help how we feel.

However, we can make thoughtful decisions about what we will do about how we feel.

In this way, children learn early on that being angry is permissible and normal. They also understand that they have choices about what they can do (other than paste the offending person in the mouth) when they do get angry. A parent can show the child that he or she is very much in control of his or her anger.

Parent: How long do you want to be angry?
Child: Ten minutes.

Parent:	How angry do you want to be?
Child:	Red angry!
Parent:	Red angry?
Child:	Well, maybe real dark pink angry.
Parent:	Okay. When you are ready to put your anger away, let me know, so we can talk about it together and figure out what you might want to do when you see Alice tomorrow.
Child:	I'll still want to paste her in the mouth.
Parent:	I understand. However, if you do that, what will Alice do?
Child:	Probably hit me back.
Parent:	And what will that accomplish?
(pregnant pause)	
Child:	I see what you mean.
Parent:	Good. So, when you are finished with being angry, let's talk about what you should do tomorrow when you see Alice.

If every person understood from early on—like age three—that he or she was in control of his or her anger, many of the random acts of hostility we see today would not occur. We need to teach our children that anger is not some strange, powerful force outside of them and entirely beyond their control. We need to show them how to *own* their anger, rather than blame it on someone else. There is a power in owning anger. It means you can calibrate it and control it in terms of duration and intensity. Teach children to say:

"I am angry," *not* "You make me angry."
"I don't like what you've said," *not* "How dare you say that to me!"
"I think that's very unkind of you," *not* "You're a dirt bag!"

When siblings are fighting, instead of the usual parental shouting that the kids "Stop that nonsense immediately!" many parents encourage their children to have a pillow fight. The pillow fight usually ends in laughter and a conflict-resolving discussion.

In a close relationship such as marriage, it is helpful if the adults have some agreed-upon strategies to unload hostility and frustration without destroying the relationship in the process. Here are methods some folks have used:

- Make an appointment for a fight—date, time, topic—and give the other person time to prepare. (In other words, in a close relationship, let there be no sneak attacks.)
- Engage in a pillow fight.
- Let both partners scream their frustration at one another simultaneously, with neither one listening to the other.
- Have each partner take one minute to scream their frustration at the other; the other must listen but must not respond.

Whichever strategy is used, after the process of unloading is complete, a rational conflict-resolving discussion must take place.

Another strategy which people use is to write a letter to the offending person. The letter is then put aside. Several days later, when the heat of the moment has passed and the person is able to look at the situation with a little more objectivity, the person reviews the letter. At that point the decision is made whether to send the letter, revise it, or simply toss it away.

In a case where the offending party is long dead and gone, psychiatric counselors have recommended the following strategy. Place two chairs opposite one another. Pretend that one chair is occupied by the (dead) offending party. You sit in the other. Close your eyes, and in your mind see the offending party sitting opposite you. Have a long mental conversation, in which you lay out all the aggravations and hostility you have been holding on to all these many years. Explain everything. When you are finished, open your eyes. You will notice that all your hostility toward that (dead) other person has disappeared. Counselors explain the phenomenon this way. If you make the conversation real enough, with passion and feeling, your mind will assume that the conversation actually took place. Your mind will assume that the offending person actually heard and absorbed everything you said.

As a society, we must take on the responsibility of teaching our children (and adults) how to confront hostility-creating incidents in their lives, so that they take appropriate action—action that will ameliorate their anger while not creating additional problems. In this way, individuals can grow up with some fundamental guidelines for managing their very legitimate hostility.

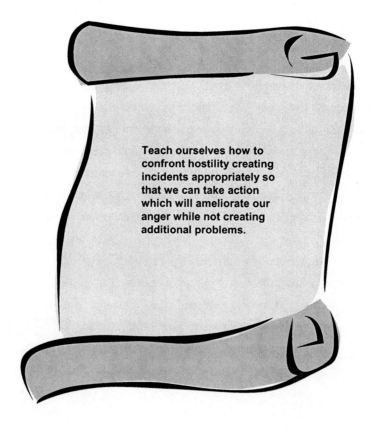

Teach ourselves how to confront hostility creating incidents appropriately so that we can take action which will ameliorate our anger while not creating additional problems.

Chapter Two Exercises

Directions: After each chapter in this book, there will be various exercises, designed both to test your knowledge about the process of conflict resolution and to shed some light on how you might choose to deal with various conflict issues. The correct answers and explanations will immediately follow the exercises.

1. If I am in conflict with someone at home or at work, it means I am a bad person.
   - True
   - False
2. Holding my aggravations and hostility inside and never talking about what is bothering me is the best way to avoid a conflict.
   - True
   - False
3. In order to prove that I am a strong person, and not a wimp, it is crucial that I confront every issue or person that causes me a problem or increase in my stress level.
   - True
   - False
4. If I attempt to discuss what the other person is doing that is causing me a problem, I will likely make things worse.
   - True
   - False

5. It is always best to start a conflict-resolving discussion by telling the other person how I think the problem might be resolved.
   - True
   - False
6. In a conflict, the person with the most power will win.
   - True
   - False
7. The other person's view of the problem is every bit as legitimate as mine.
   - True
   - False
8. If I am really very angry about some situation another person has forced upon me, my best strategy is to:
   - Say nothing; go out and get drunk.
   - Scream at my spouse about how unfair life is and how mean others can be.
   - Go to the gym and have it out with my boxing partner.
   - Read the Bible passage about turning the other cheek.
   - Get a great big club, go to the person's house, and threaten his existence if he ever does anything like that again.
   - Have a conversation with the other person and explain my side of things.
   - Show a willingness to listen to her view of the situation.
   - Look for an opportunity to get even by doing something that I know will really upset the other person.

Answers to Chapter Two Exercises

1. If I am in conflict with someone at home or at work, it means I am a bad person.

   False. This is nonsense. Conflict is a very normal occurrence when people work closely together on common goals in an interdependent manner and care very much about what goes on.

2. Holding my aggravations and hostility inside and never talking about what is bothering me is the best way to avoid a conflict.

   False. This does not make any sense. Unless you discuss the problem, no resolution is possible. Moreover, with time, your aggravations and hostility over the situation will increase. Discussing conflict issues with the person involved is the best way to make those problems go away.

3. In order to prove that I am a strong person, and not a wimp, it is crucial that I confront every issue.

   False. This is not true. You have to pick your battles. Confront the issues that bother you the most. First of all, some things are really trivial and, in the big picture, are not worth the effort. Secondly, if you confronted everything that caused you stress, you'd be a most unpopular and extremely exhausted person.

4. If I attempt to discuss what the other person is doing that is causing me a problem, I will likely make things worse.

   True. This is true, at least temporarily. Should this happen, you must attempt to have a second conflict-resolving discussion. Eventually, the other person will listen.

5. Its always best to start a conflict-resolving discussion by telling the other person how I think the problem might be resolved.

   True. Perhaps it might be better stated that you should start a conflict-resolving discussion by telling the other person how you would *like* to see the problem resolved. Just dumping a problem on the table is frustrating for most people. However, if you describe the problem and also suggest a solution, you are more likely to engage the other person in a solution-finding discussion that will satisfy both of you.

6. In a conflict, the person with the most power will win.

   False. This is not necessarily so. Power, whether it be as a result of the person's position on the organizational chart or because he or she makes the more aggressive stance, provides no guarantee of a win. It depends on how the discussion is managed and the attitude of the people involved.

7. The other person's view of the problem is every bit as legitimate as mine.

   True. Look at it this way: each of you is trying to do the best job you can with the information and skills at your disposal. Your adversary may have a perspective that you think is all wrong, but, whatever it is, it makes sense to her. Therefore, find out what piece of information you are missing that, if you had it, would help you better understand your adversary's actions.

8. If you are really very angry about some situation another person has forced upon you, the best strategy is to *have a conversation* with the other person, explain your side of things, and show a willingness to listen to her view of the situation. Remember that such a confrontation is not a battle for the planet Earth. You don't need to act like Van Weasel. Such tactics will get you an "Up yours!" from the other person.

Chapter Three

The Strategy of "Don't Get Mad, Get Even"

RATHER THAN DIRECTLY ADDRESSING THE conflict-causing issue with the other party, many people will engage in a strategy of getting even. This popular method of dealing with conflict is especially useful in situations where the aggrieved party is far less powerful than the perpetrator. It is used when a person is convinced he or she has no other viable method for dealing with the situation. It is important to remember, however, that the target of the getting-even behavior seldom gets the message. As a result, the basic problem continues.

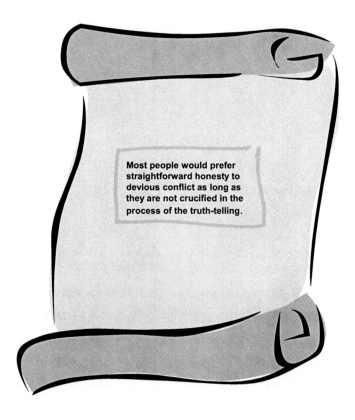

Most people would prefer straightforward honesty to devious conflict as long as they are not crucified in the process of the truth-telling.

In the family loan situation, for example, if you were trying to get even with your brother-in-law for putting pressure on your spouse to convince you to make a loan to him you might give the brother-in-law a check that is certain to bounce. Then the basic problem would surely continue!

Here is another example. A late spring snowstorm had closed the Boston airport; all flights had been delayed or canceled. A large, very aggravated businessman, toting a fold-over hanging suit bag and bulging briefcase and dragging a small wheelie suitcase behind him, stepped up to the ticket clerk and in a loud voice demanded to know when his flight was going to get off the ground. The ticket clerk, in her nicest customer service manner, smiled and patiently explained that all flights were being delayed due to the snow, and as soon as it was deemed safe the flights

...d continue. Not being satisfied with her response, the man raised his voice several decibels and exclaimed, "Because of your insane fear of a little snow, I will miss my connection. I have a critical meeting to attend in Omaha, and it's going to be your fault that I'm late, missy!"

"But, sir," she responded, "We are concerned for your safety, and as soon as flight operations notify us, you'll be on your way." The man then became abusive with the ticket clerk, calling her, among other things, a deceitful moron who was delaying his flight only until every passenger seat was occupied. Very sweetly she again explained that the situation was beyond her control, and as soon as it was safe for the flights to resume, he would be on his way.

With a mighty heave, the man launched his fold-over suit bag at the ticket clerk. This was quickly followed by his small wheelie bag. Then he tossed his ticket at her. After ducking out of the way, the clerk proceeded with the check-in process. Muttering under his breath, the man then stomped off.

A young woman was the next in line. She commiserated with the clerk. "He was so awful to you. One person like that could ruin your whole day, yet here you are smiling and doing your job just as if nothing had happened. Don't you wish you could have smacked him in the face?" "Oh, we have our ways," responded the clerk with a gleeful smile. "He's going to Omaha, but his luggage is going to Oahu."

Could the ticket clerk have spoken up to the rude customer and told him that she did not appreciate his disrespectful behavior? Probably not. Her customer service training would have advised against such action. She did not want to feel abused and helpless, so she struck back by sending her Mr. Nasty's luggage to the wrong destination. If called upon to explain the misrouted luggage, she could have sloughed it off by explaining, "Oh, my! I must have made a mistake. We were in such a turmoil with the weather delays and cancellations and all."

When people express their resentment by creating problems for the target of their annoyance, the behavior is labeled *passive-aggressive behavior*. The problem with this kind of behavior, as this situation illustrates, is that the other party seldom gets the actual message. This businessman will go away believing that his misrouted luggage was just a simple mistake made by the airlines' inept staff.

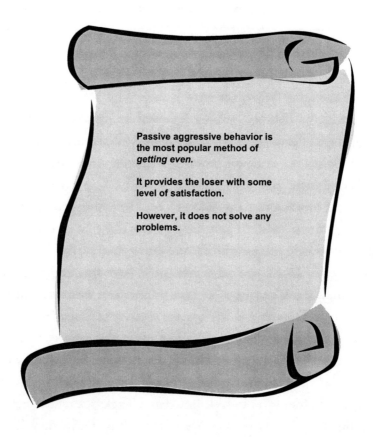

Passive aggressive behavior is the most popular method of *getting even.*

It provides the loser with some level of satisfaction.

However, it does not solve any problems.

Let's suppose that you are a young kid working on an assembly line. The union contract specifies that overtime is voluntary. Production in your area is running well behind current needs. The foreman asks if you would be willing to work overtime on the weekend to help catch up. You have other plans, so you respectfully decline his request. The foreman, in front of all your peers, manipulatively insists that you come in, by saying, "Everyone else will be here. You know how important it is to be a team player. You're not going to let us down, are you?" (This verbal strategy is known as *the guilt trip*.)

You feel exploited and angry. You mumble your unwilling agreement. On Saturday morning, bright and early, you take your place on the line, carefully making sure that everything you put together has some sort of error in it. At the end of the shift, nothing made that day passes quality control. You are delighted when you hear the foreman getting chewed out by the plant manager. "You had an entire crew here at time and a half, and not one item passed quality control! You idiot!"

The target of the passive-aggressive behavior, the foreman, doesn't really understand what actually happened. Therefore, the frustration of both parties will continue. The foreman will again use manipulative tactics when requesting overtime, and the kid will once again make junk. The kid has not learned to stand his ground, and the boss has not learned to be honest, but respectful and straightforward, with his crew members.

When one party attempts to stand his or her ground and the other party chooses to belittle or disregard the concerns of the first party, retaliation often comes in the form of a "Don't get mad, get even" reaction.

Chuck Howell was moving up quickly in his organization. His young and attractive wife, Laura, was a legendary good cook. For political reasons, Charles would often invite his widower boss to accompany him home for a gourmet dinner. The first few times, the boss behaved himself. Then Laura noticed that the boss would "accidentally" brush up against her. Several times she became aware that he was standing behind her peering down her blouse. She was becoming very uncomfortable in his presence. Laura explained the situation to her husband and asked that he not invite the boss to their home again.

Chuck:	Tom is harmless. I'm sure he didn't mean anything by it. He just finds you very attractive. I think you're being overly sensitive. I would hate to deny him the pleasure of a home-cooked dinner just because you find his behavior a little offensive. Besides, your great dinners have certainly enhanced my chances for promotion.
Laura:	Let me get this straight. You want me to ignore the fact that this man, a guest in my home, someone who is eating food that I prepared, is making me uncomfortable? You want me to endure his insulting behavior, so you can grease your promotional wheels?
Chuck:	Look, sweetheart, I'm only doing this for us. Surely you can overlook Tom's supposed bad manners for a few hours once a month. It could mean more money for us.

Although Laura continued to press for no more invitations for old Tom, her husband ignored her pleas. Tom was invited for another dinner the following month.

Now, Tom was a meat and potatoes sort of guy. He was not fond of fish or chicken in any form, and he disliked most vegetables. So, for his next visit, Laura fixed a creamed chicken casserole with mashed cauliflower served over white rice. She even borrowed her neighbor's plain white dishes on which to serve the meal.

Tom nearly vomited when she placed his dinner plate before him. What made it worse was that Laura gave him a big smile and an unwavering straight-in-the-eyeball look as she asked, "How do you like my casserole?" Tom felt forced to eat it. Soon, the only color at the table was Tom's green pallor. That was the last time Tom accepted an invitation to dinner. When Chuck questioned his wife on her choice of entrée, she explained that the meat in the supermarket hadn't looked fresh and the chicken was being offered at a great bargain.

Passive-aggressive behavior is a strategy of attacking and getting even without actually addressing the target of one's dissatisfaction. It happens everywhere. For example, in a busy supermarket, there is usually one checkout with a sign limiting the number of items. The sign reads "12 items or less." When a woman with a very full grocery cart muscles her way into this line, we can observe a variety of passive aggressive reactions.

One person in the line angrily shouts, "Hey, lady, can't you read?"

Another turns to the person behind her and says, "Did you see what she did?"

Another lady sighs loudly and addresses the air above her head, saying, "Some people are *sooo* pushy."

Another shopper reaches into the candy display alongside the grocery line and dumps several trays of candy and gum into the woman's already overflowing grocery cart.

Apparently it is easier to engage in hostile behaviors than it is to simply say, "Excuse me, ma'am, you're in the wrong line. This is the checkout line for *twelve items or less*. Please move to a different line."

To stand one's ground while confronting another person is uncomfortable. Whether it be a spouse, child, co-worker, boss, or a stranger in the supermarket, we are certain that we will incur the resentment and hostility of the other person. Certainly, we will also generate feelings of anxiety in ourselves. We might make the decision, therefore, to do nothing at all about the situation. We tell ourselves that this was a very minor aggravation. Live with it. Move on, we tell ourselves. Psychologically, however, we cannot simply *move on*. The situation replays in our minds over and over and over. At every replay, our stress increases. Why? Because, deep down inside, we believe we should have *done something* to avoid leaving the situation feeling like a loser.

Take the common event of someone beating you out of a parking space in a very crowded parking lot. Suppose he gives you a nasty smile and a hand gesture of triumph. Although you move on to seek another parking space, you boil inside a little. That person took advantage of you in a way that left you unable to fight back. Filled with unresolved hostility, you fantasize about taking the air out of his tires or parking in such a way as to block him in. Maybe you consider painting the back window with black spray paint or putting a little sugar into the gas tank.

Your distress doesn't end there. You tell the next three people you run into the story of your parking lot catastrophe. Why do you do that? There isn't a person on the planet to whom this has not happened. Why should you feel compelled to tell and retell the story? It is because you are trying to rationalize your non-response to the situation. Deep down you believe you should have done something to take back control of the situation. Somehow, you should have made it work out so that you did not come off feeling like such a deficient human being. You have, however, no idea of what that might be.

The circumstances of the supermarket line and the parking lot space involve strangers; people you are not likely to run into again. Suppose, however, close friends or co-workers put you in an emotionally similar situation where, again, you are left feeling that you are a deficient human being, because you should have done something to take back control of the situation. Somehow, you should have made it work out right.

For example, imagine that you and your spouse are having dinner at the home of some very close friends. During the hors d'oeuvres, the other couple begins to take potshots at one another. By the time the main course is on the table, your hosts are into a full-blown argument. You and your spouse are extremely uncomfortable, especially when you are invited to side with one or the other. You inhale the meal and depart as quickly as possible. On the way home, you ask each other if you should have done something other than run away. Perhaps you should have said something—but what? Once again, the situation has left you and your spouse feeling used and deficient.

Suppose you are at a business meeting with your boss and peers. One of your peers puts the blame for a recent screw-up squarely on your shoulders by erroneously describing what took place. If you say, "That's not what happened," or "I did no such thing," you will be taking a weak, defensive posture. So you ask yourself, "What should I do? What should I say?"

Since this takes place in front of everyone with whom you work, you decide to explain things privately to the boss later on. But this action does not resolve things for you. You sit up half the night thinking up things you should have said or done to take back control of the situation. The fact that you did nothing leaves you feeling angry, used, abused, embarrassed, and inept. You begin to consider how you might get even with your co-worker for his unwarranted attack.

You come up with a great plan. Your company is one of five in a specialized technical business. All the CEOs in these five businesses know one another and have agreed not to steal one another's highly trained staff members. Furthermore, they have also agreed to immediately terminate any staff person at any one of the companies who seeks a position for more money at one of the other companies.

Your co-worker keeps an updated resume on his computer. So, very early one morning, you sneak into his cubicle, download his resume and send it to the CEOs of the other four companies. The cover letter you send with the resume states, "I am seeking a position with greater responsibility that is commensurate with my experience and an increase in salary that will reflect a greater appreciation of my technical expertise." One week later, your co-worker is summarily terminated. You feel happily justified. You leveled the playing field. Your co-worker, however, has no idea how or why his resume got into the hands of the other organizations.

It has always been a source of amazement to me how far people will go to avoid talking to the offending party and attempting to resolve their problems. Somehow, the *"Don't get mad, get even"* approach always appears to be the more attractive strategy.

Ken and Marie were madly in love when they married and set up housekeeping in a small cottage. Almost immediately, his mother manipulated her way into their tiny household. She missed her only child and convinced her son that she would be an asset, helping with the cooking and cleaning.

From the very beginning, there were problems. If husband and wife were discussing the color scheme for the living room, Mama would get into the middle of the discussion, and, before long, the couple would be arguing about the color of the drapes. If Ken and Marie were talking about establishing a savings program or an insurance limit on their homeowners' policy, there was Mama, right in the thick of things, telling the couple what they should do. Inevitably, Ken and Marie would get into an argument over Mama's ideas.

The couple realized that if they didn't do something drastic, and do it soon, their once-happy marriage was headed for the rocks. So, they put their little home up for sale. They explained to Mama that they really could not afford a house at this time. In the process, they took a sizable loss on the house. Then they moved into a tiny apartment—where there was absolutely no room for Mama.

The couple lived happily in their tight quarters for two years. Then Marie discovered she was pregnant. The couple recognized that there was no room in their tiny apartment for them and a baby. Once again, they went house-hunting. Now, of course, they were presented with the problem of Mama wanting to move in to "help with the baby."

At this point, Ken and Marie sought professional help. They explained to the psychologist that they both felt under tremendous pressure. He was contemplating moving his little family to Alaska (Mama hated cold weather). Marie was threatening to abort the child if Mama was going to become a part of their little household.

Marie and Ken solved the problem by attending a workshop in Assertive Communication. Together they developed a brief speech, which Ken delivered to his mother over the telephone.

"Mother, although Marie and I appreciate your desire to live with us, we have decided that it is not a wise decision. It makes us feel uncomfortable to deny your request, because we both love you. We want you to plan for a short five-day visit, after the baby is born. That would work so much better for us in terms of stress. How does that sound to you?"

Passive-aggressive behavior is not the way to resolve a conflict, nor is running away. You must speak up and address the situation and the aggravation immediately in a calm and respectful manner. The process can be learned. This book will give you strategies for managing both your own and other people's emotionality. Never again will you have to sacrifice your self-esteem or endure the disrespect of another person. Being able to keep a composed demeanor in the face of infuriating situations will enable you to quickly move on to conflict resolution. This ability will alleviate many of the daily tensions and stresses that often make life so difficult. This is the key to personal power. It is also the secret to conflict resolution—because it leaves no one feeling defeated and desiring reprisal.

Chapter Three Exercises

Directions: For questions 1, 2, and 5, checkmark the best response. For questions 3, 4, 6, 7 and 8 indicate true or false. Answers and explanations follow.

1. Which of the following statements is true? It is not possible for two people involved in a conflict to communicate:
   - without emotions getting in the way
   - without someone saying something they will regret later
   - frankly and honestly without offending one another
   - clearly and accurately so as to avoid any misinterpretation
   - without getting others involved in their dispute
   - without other petty or unrelated issues slipping into the discussion
   - without someone taking an inflexible position and becoming bullheaded

2. The most important skill in conflict management and resolution is:
   - listening
   - emotional self-control
   - asking good questions
   - being open-minded and receptive
   - flexibility
   - a sense of humor

3. When you know the other person is the one creating the problem, you should tell them right off what they are doing wrong and why they should change their actions.
   - True
   - False

4. People who are passive-aggressive are secretly extremely angry.
   - True
   - False

5. When dealing with conflict, the old saying "Go along to get along" really means:
   - Don't make a big deal out of something unimportant.
   - You should just live with the problem and not make waves.
   - You have to look for cunning, indirect ways to solve your problems.
   - Around here it's simply not wise to openly disagree with anyone.
   - The person speaking has no strategy for conflict resolution.

6. In a conflict-resolving discussion, the party with the most flexibility will win.
   - True
   - False

7. The more you ruminate about a conflict situation, the better and more creative are the ideas you come up with for handling it.
   - True
   - False

8. Facing up to conflict is difficult, because it is actually three separate issues rolled up into one.
   - True
   - False

Answers to Chapter Three Exercises

1. All are true. It is not possible for two people involved in a conflict to communicate frankly and honestly without offending one another. Remember, however, that most people would prefer a little straightforward honesty to negative undercurrents and conflict, as long as they are not insulted or otherwise crucified in the process of the truth-telling. As a matter of fact, once the problem is out on the table, you are very likely to hear, "Oh my. I wasn't aware that you _____. I only wish you had said something about this sooner."

2. The most important skill in conflict management and resolution is *listening*. In order to resolve a conflict, both parties must know exactly where the other person stands on the issue. That only comes about if the combatants listen to one another. All the other items listed are good skills to have as well, but listening is the most critical skill.

3. When you know the other person is the one creating the problem, you should tell him right off what he is doing and why he should change his actions. **True**. However, you have to be careful how you characterize the problem. First of all, do not start with the word *you*. Instead, begin by saying something like, "I'm having a problem with such and such a situation, and only you can help me sort it out." Often your adversary is totally unaware that he is creating difficulties for you by acting or behaving the way he is. You want to raise awareness, not attack the person with criticism.

In addition, always remember to explain not only the *what*, but also the *why*. When we respect another person we explain both; when we do not respect the other person, we speak only of the *what*.

4. People who are passive-aggressive are secretly extremely angry. This is **true**. People who engage in passive-aggressive behavior are holding on to a good deal of unexpressed anger. These are the people who live by the axiom, "Don't get mad, get even."

    This behavior is seen frequently in the work setting, when individuals fear that speaking their minds might result in negative consequences or a loss of employment. These are the people who engage in actions purposefully designed to annoy the target of their anger. They then claim it was just a simple mistake or oversight, while the target of their anger quietly seethes. It is a subtle form of reprisal. This happens in close personal relationships as well, especially when one partner uses a verbally or physically aggressive stance with the other.

5. When dealing with conflict, the old saying "Go along to get along" really means you should just *live with the problem and not make waves*. If the conflict issue is truly important to you, the result of dealing with the problem in this way is that you are left feeling used, taken advantage of, and very angry. You might even seek to address the problem by engaging in passive-aggressive behavior. If the issue is important to you, go ahead and make waves. Your own mental health should come first, the maintenance of a cordial relationship second.

6. In a conflict-resolution discussion, the person with the most flexibility will win. **True.** If you remain flexible, especially when looking at alternatives, you will always come away with *something* of what you want. If you are intractable, there's a 95 percent chance you will get *nothing* of what you want. Reasonableness begets reasonableness.

7. The more you ruminate about a conflict situation, the better and more creative are the ideas you come up with for handling it. **False.** The longer you turn over the problem in your mind, the more violent

become your mental images about dealing with your adversary, and the more extensive, hopeless, and bleak your sense of the situation becomes.

8. Facing up to conflict is difficult, because it is actually three separate issues rolled up into one. **True.** There is nothing simple about conflict. It is convoluted, complex, confusing, and untidy—because it actually embodies three problems: the issue itself; how to address the issue; and to whom you should speak regarding the issue. The answers to those three items must be determined before you attempt resolution.

Chapter Four

―――――

The Nature of Conflict

MOST PEOPLE WOULD RATHER HAVE a root canal than attempt to resolve a conflict. In fact, instead of going through the tough work of routing out the real issue and figuring out how to confront the offending party, most people will say, "Oh, it's just a personality conflict." It is never *just* a personality conflict. That's an excuse.

Every person brings to every situation unique information gleaned from their own experience, perceptions, values, and goals. In any situation that involves more than one person, there are bound to be differences of opinion. Therefore, the potential for conflict exists. The conflict is not because of personality differences but because the people involved think differently, perceive things differently, and/or have different goals.

Let's look in on a badly matched married couple. Sarah is a second generation American whose family practiced extreme frugality in order to provide the bare basics. Alex's family has deep roots in the American culture, and, as a child, he never wanted for anything. When Sarah shops, she purchases the cheapest cuts of meat; when Alex does the shopping, he buys the most expensive cuts. Sarah makes wonderful meals from leftovers. Alex hates leftovers, even when they are disguised as a creative casserole. When mechanical items break down, Alex throws out the broken item and replaces it with a new one. Sarah will take the broken item to be fixed. She tells him, "It's important to save for a rainy day. You never know what might happen." Alex tells Sarah, "Life is short. We only go this way once. We should enjoy all that our money can do for us right now." Sarah thinks Alex is wasteful and reckless. Alex thinks Sarah is anal and compulsive. Instead of each of them acting as if the other is totally wrong, this couple should explore the reasons why each looks at the world from such a different perspective.

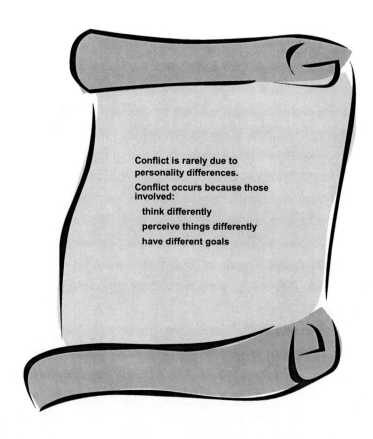

Conflict is rarely due to personality differences.

Conflict occurs because those involved:

   think differently

   perceive things differently

   have different goals

Here is a work example. Suppose you are the manager of the Design Department, and your opponent is the manager of the Accounting Department. *Your* goals are about designing the best, most efficient edge-of-technology gizmos in the marketplace. Your *opponent's* goals are concerned with keeping the costs of manufacturing down so that the price of the gizmos is competitive in the marketplace.

You have designed a new, fantastic gizmo model. Retooling to accommodate your new design will be far more expensive than just continuing to produce last year's standard model gizmo. However, producing last year's standard gizmo model renders your department unnecessary. When your opponent doesn't want to spend the money, you might conclude that the Accounting Manager dislikes you personally and is devising clever ways to get rid of you. You might also assume that you are focusing on the future in order to keep the company ahead of the technological curve, while the Accounting Manager is just an old fuddy-duddy who wants to hang on to old ways of doing things.

Neither assessment is true. What you have here is a simple conflict over goals. It is not personal. Moreover, it requires that those at the level above you determine what the company should produce and bring to the marketplace in the coming year—a brand-new model gizmo or more of the older model.

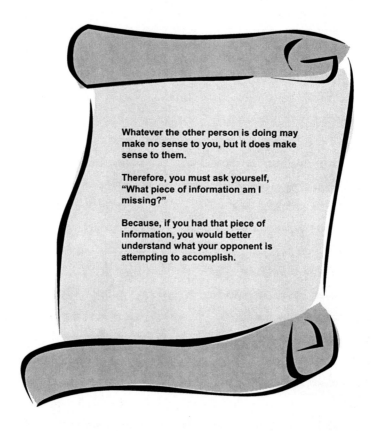

Whatever the other person is doing may make no sense to you, but it does make sense to them.

Therefore, you must ask yourself, "What piece of information am I missing?"

Because, if you had that piece of information, you would better understand what your opponent is attempting to accomplish.

In the gizmo's case, you are missing a critical piece of information. The CFO told the Accounting Manager that manufacturing expenses had to be trimmed 12 percent in the coming year. The estimated increase for retooling the manufacturing process to accommodate your new model gizmo is 16 percent. This would result in the Accounting Manager having to trim 38 percent from the manufacturing costs. It would be impossible for him to do that. Therefore, in order to accomplish his goal of trimming 12 percent from manufacturing costs, the Accounting Manager feels forced to avoid incurring any additional manufacturing costs, including those for retooling. Therefore, he feels compelled to take a position against your new design.

Whatever the other person is doing may make no sense to you, but it does make sense to him. Therefore, you must ask yourself, "What piece of information am I missing that, if I had it, would help me understand what my opponent is attempting to accomplish?"

The first thing you should understand about conflict is that it is a perfectly normal occurrence between human beings. It is not necessarily good, nor is it necessarily bad. It is just a very common by-product of people working and living together.

The second thing you should know about conflict is that it can only occur when people care about what's going on. If nobody gives a hoot about how things are done, who is doing what, and which things are more important than other things, there is no conflict. However, if you and your adversary are personally invested in what's happening, and you both care about doing what's right and doing it in the right way, you will inevitably find yourselves in a conflict.

Imagine, for example, that a couple has a young child with a huge nose. The mother wants the child to undergo corrective surgery immediately. The father believes it would be better to wait until the child is older and can better tolerate the operation. During her childhood, the mother was severely teased, because she was taller than any of her classmates. When she remembers her grade-school years, the pain of the teasing comes back to her full force. She doesn't want her child to go through what she went through. It could, she believes, scar him for life. The father, on the other hand, was never taunted during his early school years. Therefore, he is certain that his child will be able to successfully ignore any teasing.

This is not a matter of who is right and who is wrong. Both positions have merit. What needs to happen here is, instead of arguing, these parents need to share where their views of the situation come from. Both need to acknowledge that each wants the best for their child. Next, they need to consult the child's doctor about the age and surgery-tolerance issue. Finally, they need to examine their child's reaction to being teased. The child's history—not the parents' history—should determine when or if such corrective surgery will take place.

Suppose that management has assigned you and a co-worker three projects, which you must work on together. You think that project Buick should be done before project Chevy. Your co-worker thinks that project Ford should be handled before either Buick or Chevy. Understand that neither of you is wrong. You just see the situation differently. Furthermore, both of you probably have other regular work priorities for which you are responsible. Those must be accomplished as well. In order to work on these extra projects, both of you will need to coordinate your time and be cooperative in your efforts, remembering that whatever one of you does regarding Buick, Chevy, and Ford will inevitably be affected by what the other does. This situation is ripe for conflict. Not only might you be in conflict because you care about the order of how and when the work is accomplished, you might also be in conflict because you have to coordinate your time and activities for both your regular work and the project work.

On the other hand, pretend for a moment that you and a co-worker are both college professors at the same institution. You are the head of the Chemistry Department and your colleague is the head of the Literature Department. Would you really care if your colleague decided to add a course in Russian literature? Would your colleague have a problem if you decided to add a course in nuclear chemistry? Absolutely not! In such a situation, even though you both are employed by the same organization, you do not work together, nor are you interdependent in any way. You have your own budget and your colleague has hers. You have your staff and your colleague has hers. Each of you makes your own decisions without having to consider what the other is doing. Therefore, there is no possibility of conflict.

In a marriage, conflict occurs precisely because whatever one does inevitably affects the other. The couple is interdependent. Moreover, both care about what's going on. Both are concerned about doing things right and deciding which things are more important than other things. They are personally invested in what goes on in their lives.

Returning to the college example, let's say there is a limited amount of building funds available. The Chemistry Department needs a new laboratory. The Literature Department wants a new wing built onto the library. These demands have all the makings for a serious conflict. Those involved in the sciences will side with the Chemistry Department, while those involved in the Liberal Arts side of the university will side with the Literature Department. Since there is not enough money to fulfill both needs, there will be conflict. People will question whether the institution should make its primary focus liberal arts or concentrate on the sciences. The alumnae will get involved, because they are the ones who endow the institution. As you can see, we now have a full-blown conflict situation, with many different interests involved.

Much of the work in today's world is accomplished through teams—small groups of people working together to accomplish specific goals. The assumption is that if management brings a number of skilled people together and unites them behind some very specific goals, the work will go forward magically, smoothly, and effectively.

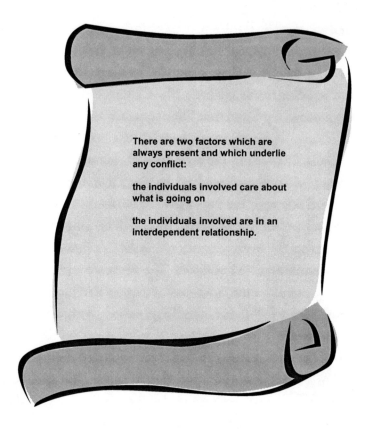

There are two factors which are always present and which underlie any conflict:

the individuals involved care about what is going on

the individuals involved are in an interdependent relationship.

Often, things don't go so *smoothly*, because one or more persons in the group is not fully invested in what the group is doing. Perhaps he or she didn't want to be a part of this team in the first place. It may be that there are too many other, more critical, work responsibilities awaiting his or her attention. Maybe the person had hopes of being team leader, and when someone else was selected, he or she became bitter. Whatever the reason, that person might decide—on purpose—to create difficulties for the group by not doing their share of the work or not doing their share well.

Twenty-five managers were participating in a five-day training course on leadership. Each day, after the lessons and lectures, there would be a game, which was designed to help secure the learning of the day. One of the teams of five had decided to round-robin the role of leader so that each member of the team would have a chance to play boss for a day. This particular team was very successful with the games. They handily beat the other teams on Monday, Tuesday, and Wednesday.

On Thursday, the lessons revolved around team leadership, team management, team building, and self-managing teams. The game of the day involved building a helicopter out of Lego pieces. The team who had initially decided to round-robin the leadership role now changed their strategy. They determined that in order to continue their fantastic winning streak, they could not afford to allow the next person in line, Phil, to take the leadership role. Phil was the least experienced in the group when it came to managing. Therefore, the team members decided to call upon Carl, who had done a spectacular leadership job with Tuesday's game, to be boss once again.

Although Phil was furious, he said nothing. The game commenced, and, as usual, Carl's team finished first—way ahead of the other teams. When looking at the blueprints, however, the team could easily see that the helicopter they had made did not quite resemble the blueprints. Carl quickly instructed the team to take their model apart and start over. Once again the team finished their task before the other teams, and once again, their model did not match the blueprints.

"Perhaps," one team member said in desperation, "There's a piece missing." Once again the team tore their helicopter apart. This time they began by counting the parts and comparing their totals with the totals listed on the parts list. At this point, the other teams were completing their helicopters. All of their copters were constructed correctly. "We're going to lose," Carl cried out. "I don't believe this; we're the fastest team and we're actually going to lose. How could this happen?"

At this point, Phil leaned back in his chair, a triumphant grin on his face, and held out his hand. There, nestled in his palm, was a crucial piece. "See, I fixed you guys," he said. The team was crushed. Although they fully understood what had happened and why it had happened, their motivation for further participation in the workshop was over. Nothing could regenerate their enthusiasm. Phil's single act of reprisal against the team for not allowing him to be team leader in the exercise destroyed the group's ability to achieve the completion of the exercise. Moreover, Phil's attempt at *getting even* also prevented the team from continuing to function as a successful group.

The point here is that when people work interdependently, each individual involved has the power and ability to make things difficult for all the others involved. This is the basis for much of the conflict that arises at work. The same is true for a marriage; each partner has equal power and ability to destroy the relationship.

When people work interdependently (like a marriage or a work team), each person has equal power and ability to make things difficult for all the others involved.

Each also has equal power to destroy the team's ability to function successfully.

Chapter Four Exercises

Directions: If the responses to the following questions seem obvious to you, you are making great progress toward becoming proficient at conflict resolution.

1. Attempting to talk things out is always a good first step when trying to resolve a conflict.
   - True
   - False

2. Conflict is neither good nor bad. It just is.
   - True
   - False

3. There's only one possible result in a conflict: one person goes away the winner; the other goes away the loser.
   - True
   - False

4. Around here, there is a history of people being reprimanded, tortured, beaten, and even fired for attempting to resolve a conflict.
   - True
   - False

5. When attempting to resolve a conflict, it is critical to keep personalities and emotions out of the process and to focus only on the facts.
    - True
    - False

6. If you want to prevail in a conflict, a good strategy is to put the other party on the defensive as quickly as possible.
    - True
    - False

7. Whether the outcome of a conflict situation is positive or negative is almost totally determined by the way in which it is handled.
    - True
    - False

8. The basic reason why two people might find themselves in a serious conflict is personality differences.
    - True
    - False

Answers to Chapter Four Exercises

1. Attempting to talk things out is always a good first step. **This is true.** So often the other person has no idea that he or she has created difficulties for you. The problem might be immediately resolved when you explain the situation.

    If the conversation doesn't do the trick, you always have the option of escalating your attempt to solve the problem by bringing in other parties. However, if you begin by bringing other parties in—such as a neighbor, your mother, personnel, or your manager—the resolution process is no longer in your hands. Moreover, once other people are involved, you cannot go back to the more simple one-on-one discussion.

2. Conflict, in and of itself, is neither good nor bad. **This is true.** We make conflict a bad thing by how we talk and think about it. In actuality, conflict is a common and natural consequence of people working and living interdependently who are tied together by mutual goals in which they have a personal stake.

3. There's only one possible result in a conflict: one person goes away ... **This is false.** The only time one person goes away the winner and the other leaves as the loser is when one of the combatants utilizes a win-lose strategy. The win-lose outcome is the one outcome you want to avoid, because the loser will be looking for an opportunity to get even later on. There are four other strategies you can use in conflict resolution to secure a win-win solution. Win-win solutions mean both of you leave the discussion having gained something of what you wanted and an outcome you can live with.

4. Around here there is a history of people being reprimanded, tortured … **Hopefully, this is false**. If you are a person who really hates even the thought of confronting another person, this is probably one of the horror stories you tell yourself. It provides a justification for not trying to resolve the problem. It often helps to ask yourself, "What's the worst that can happen?" Then, take the answer you get and trim it down 75 percent. In this way, "He'll probably kill me!" becomes "He'll probably look at me like I'm nuts."

5. When attempting to resolve a conflict, it is critical to keep personalities and emotions out of the process. **This is true.** It is, however, extremely difficult to do. Perhaps the best you can hope to do is maximize the attention you give to the facts and minimize the concern you focus on the personalities and emotions of the situation. One famous negotiator put it this way: "Be tough on the problems and easy on the people." Always remember that using logic to change people's *feelings* never works. That is because feelings are emotional, not logical. Working logically with the *facts*, however, will provide a greater chance of success.

6. If you want to prevail in a conflict, a good strategy is to put the other party on the defensive. **This is false.** Putting people on the defensive may make you feel powerful, but it is certainly no way to encourage problem-solving. You both need one another's help and willing participation in the exercise in order to find a win-win solution.

7. Whether the outcome of a conflict situation is positive or negative depends on the way it is handled. **This is true.** You should always maintain a reasonable stance. Practice what you intend to say to your adversary. Make sure that your opening words are not critical, argumentative, insulting, or designed to engage your adversary's anger. You want to encourage his or her interest in problem-solving.

   Threats and verbal attacks may make a person sound really powerful on television, but that's fantasy. If your adversary is a co-worker, your conflict is just one situation in what will be a lifetime of situations with this person. Burning your bridges on this one issue just might not be the wisest thing you could do. You want an outcome that will not generate a desire for reprisal from the other person. You also want an outcome that the other person will be willing to support.

8. The basic reason why two people might find themselves in a serious conflict is mostly due to personality differences. **This is false**. In fact, nine times out of ten, conflict is due to the fact that the people involved think differently, perceive things from an alternate point of view, have dissimilar goals, or are operating on divergent information. This is why talking things out first is a good plan—it lets you know where the other person is coming from.

Chapter Five

Determining the Basis or Foundation of a Conflict

THE KEY TO MANAGING CONFLICT is to focus on the issues, not on the personalities or people involved. The goal is to reconcile different ideas or perceptions, so that mutual goals and objectives can be met. In order to do that, however, you need to understand how you came to be in a conflict in the first place. That means you must determine the primary cause of the difficulty. Most often, the cause of such difficulties lies in the *structure*, or format, under which you and the other person are functioning.

Perhaps you and the other party have overlapping responsibilities, and so neither of you is sure who should be doing what. Your co-worker Harriet says you should be doing the research, while she does the writing. You think it is the other way around. Your wife Jessie thinks you ought to take out the garbage; you think that chore is part of housecleaning and is therefore her responsibility.

Maybe neither of you is clear regarding what is expected. Although your roles are clearly delineated, you disagree about outcomes and deliverables. What both of you are supposed to accomplish is ambiguous. You think the boss wants an outline of the problem and several recommendations for resolution. Your co-worker Steve is certain the boss wants a full-blown research report detailing the root causes of the problem. Your wife Cassie thinks you ought to spend some quality time with the children each night; you believe that quality time refers to the weekend when you're not so tired and out of sorts.

EXPLORING the STRUCTURE of CONFLICT

Is there agreement regarding:

your roles?

expectations & outcomes?

means & methods for proceeding?

which facts & sources will be used?

the interpretation of the facts?

not allowing previous experiences to shape one's view of the facts?

not letting a difference in values about right & wrong interfere?

Means or methods can be another source of conflict. David wants to research replacement windows on the internet and in magazines such as Consumer Reports; Vicky wants to go with the recommendation of the window expert at the Home Depot. At work, Stanley thinks your project should be accomplished one way, and you believe some other way is better. You want to interview the people affected by the proposed project in order to gain a clearer understanding of what is needed. Your teammate Frank wants to examine the archives to learn how similar projects were accomplished in the past.

The two of you might have opposing views on the same issue, and that could be the source of your conflict. Perhaps each of you had access to a different set of facts or a different amount of information. Maybe your co-worker's information came from a seasoned, experienced employee, while yours came from the department manager, who is relatively new to the organization. Maybe your facts and information are identical but, being different individuals, you have interpreted the facts differently.

Suppose you have been working at the company for some years and are able to make certain inferences regarding certain facts. Moreover, you are also able to assign a different level of importance to some of those facts. Because your co-worker, Grace, is new to the organization, she is unable to read anything into the facts. Grace will therefore regard all the facts as equally important and take them all at face value.

It may be that you and the other person have had experience working in different areas of the organization. Therefore, even though you both might have the same facts, your perspectives are different. For example, the boss wants a fast turnaround. Your co-worker Harvey comes from sales and marketing, and for him a fast turnaround is three days. You come from research, where a fast turnaround might mean three months.

How to Analyze a Conflict

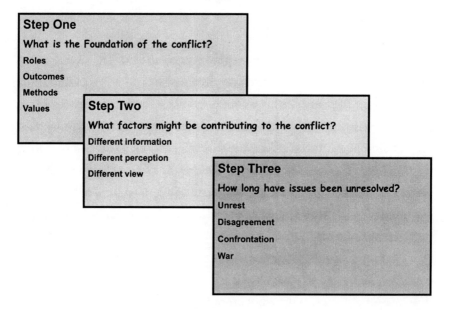

Step One

What is the Foundation of the conflict?

Roles

Outcomes

Methods

Values

Step Two

What factors might be contributing to the conflict?

Different information

Different perception

Different view

Step Three

How long have issues been unresolved?

Unrest

Disagreement

Confrontation

War

In resolving a conflict with a neighbor, your spouse wants to get advice from a lawyer relative; you want to speak with the local police department. Perhaps you believe this is a one-time problem, but your spouse wants to ensure that the issue never again comes up. Your spouse wants to sue the neighbor; you want the police to have a word with your neighbor and leave it at that.

Let's say a wife wants to put a sizable amount of the family's savings into the stock market, so that their money can grow exponentially, while keeping ahead of the rate of inflation. The husband wants to put their savings into government bonds, which are slow-growing but much safer than the stock market.

A handyman tells his homeowner-customer "I'm taking off for lunch, and I'll be back soon." To the homeowner, this means the handyman should return in one hour. The handyman, however, has a few errands to run and several phone calls to make, all involving the setting up of his next job. Lunchtime for him doesn't mean eating; it is a time for working. To him, *soon* might mean the following day.

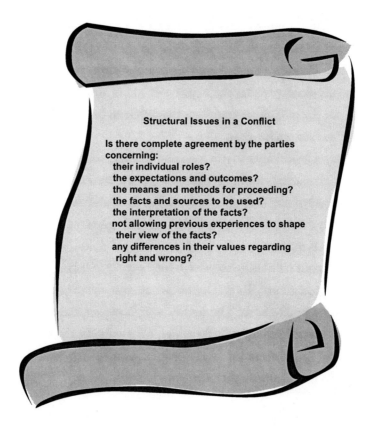

Structural Issues in a Conflict

Is there complete agreement by the parties concerning:
- **their individual roles?**
- **the expectations and outcomes?**
- **the means and methods for proceeding?**
- **the facts and sources to be used?**
- **the interpretation of the facts?**
- **not allowing previous experiences to shape their view of the facts?**
- **any differences in their values regarding right and wrong?**

Lastly, you and another person might be in conflict over values—about what is right and fair versus what is what is wrong and unacceptable. One of you might feel that in order to complete the project on time some margin for error is permissible. The other might believe that one should strive for a no-error, quality result—and if that makes the project late, so be it.

A woman might want the family to attend church every Sunday; her husband might believe that attending once each month is sufficient. Playing with the children on the weekends and involving them in family outings and other fun activities is much more important to him.

Your next step in your examination of the foundation or basis of a conflict is to look at the stage of your conflict—how long things have been left to simmer without discussion or attempts at resolution.

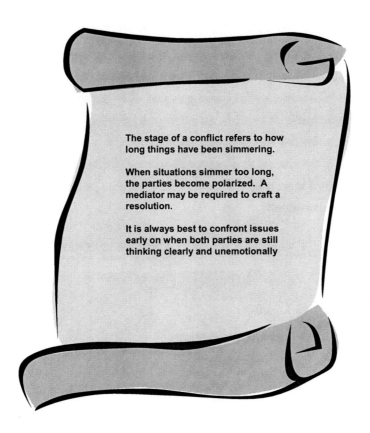

The stage of a conflict refers to how long things have been simmering.

When situations simmer too long, the parties become polarized. A mediator may be required to craft a resolution.

It is always best to confront issues early on when both parties are still thinking clearly and unemotionally

The stage of the conflict refers to how long things have been simmering. When situations are left to simmer too long, the parties become polarized. Resolution then is nearly impossible. The use of a third party—a mediator— may be necessary to find a resolution. It is always best to confront issues early on, when both parties are still thinking clearly and unemotionally.

Perhaps you and the other party are only at a situation of *unrest*. Tension is building, and both of you have a sense of impending trouble. The next stage would be *open disagreement*, when both of you are seeking information and attempting to clarify the specific issues involved. Discussions between you have begun.

The next stage would be *confrontation*, when each of you states your differences directly and clearly to the other. Each of you now has a clear vision of where the other stands. If your differences are not resolved at this stage, you move to a final stage of *open conflict*. Here, unfortunately, each of you has become ossified in your particular position. Moreover, each of you has probably gathered supporters to bolster your point of view, in an attempt to control the situation. This last stage is similar to open warfare. Obviously, it is best to deal with a conflict at the unrest or disagreement stage. When situations are left to simmer too long, and the parties have become polarized, resolution is nearly impossible.

HOW LONG HAVE ISSUES BEEN LEFT UNRESOLVED

Imagine that you and a colleague are in a conflict but have had the good sense to discuss the problem early on (the unrest stage). During your discussion, you discover that the two of you have structural differences, such as using information from different sources in approaching a shared work assignment. Rather than embarking on an attempt to influence one another as to whose information is more reliable and righteous, both of you decide to confer with the person who delegated the assignment. Your boss quickly clarifies the information issue and, like magic, your conflict goes away.

The husband and wife who are in conflict over investing their savings might talk to a financial planner. The wife will then learn that in the stock market investments never grow exponentially—and that it is also possible to lose everything. The husband will learn that government bonds, although safe, will offer little growth and also put their savings beyond their reach for a predetermined amount of time.

When you seek the assistance of someone in clarifying a structural problem, provide them with a *sufficient amount of information* so that he or she can clearly see what the differences are between the information you have and that which the other person has. The same would be true of any other structural conflict issue. Most often, a conflict arising from a structural issue simply requires clarification from a person one level above you and your co-worker (if at work) or a specialist/expert on the topic (if outside of work). It cannot be resolved at your level. You will waste time and energy trying. In addition, you will only create more hostility. The reason is that neither of you is wrong. Both of you are working in a fog, created by a lack of crucial information or someone else's unintended lack of clarity.

For instance, if you and a colleague are in conflict over values, such as delivering a quick result with some errors versus a later result with no errors, and you try to resolve this difference on your own, there will very likely be terms flying around which will not forward the problem-solving effort. These will be terms such as slipshod, compulsive, shoddy, obsessive, careless, task-oriented, expedient, overzealous, irresponsible, inflexible, and incompetent.

Neither party is wrong. The structural problem—which only the boss can resolve—is a lack of clarity regarding outcomes or deliverables. A discussion around values—who is right and who is wrong—will serve no purpose except to make working together virtually impossible. Go see the boss, and find out what she wants.

Likewise, the couple in conflict over church attendance might go speak with their pastor. They might learn that using Sundays for family activities is just as powerful for building decent, moral, respectful, and well-adjusted kids as attending church (as long as the family comes to church regularly).

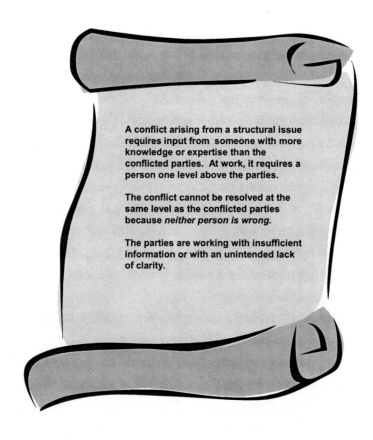

A conflict arising from a structural issue requires input from someone with more knowledge or expertise than the conflicted parties. At work, it requires a person one level above the parties.

The conflict cannot be resolved at the same level as the conflicted parties because *neither person is wrong.*

The parties are working with insufficient information or with an unintended lack of clarity.

Chapter Five Exercises

Directions: Complete the following statements. As always, the answers follow directly after the exercise.

1. Conflict is bound to occur when people work _____ and they _____.
2. In regard to the stage of a conflict, the most important issue in terms of resolution is to _____.
3. Since basis for most conflicts is structural, the parties involved should be prepared to seek _____.
4. In a conflict that is structurally based, it is critical that the parties involved spend time examining such issues as _____ before they attempt any problem-solving.
5. Conflict is absolutely unavoidable; it is a _____ of people actively living and working together.
6. The longer a conflict goes unaddressed and unresolved, the more _____ it is to resolve.
7. What makes conflict so very difficult is that it is really three separate problems masquerading as one: I _____ II _____ III _____.
8. When the basis for a conflict is structural, what makes it impossible to resolve at the level of the parties involved is that neither person is _____

Answers to Chapter Five Exercises

1. Conflict is bound to occur when people work **interdependently** and they **care about what is going on**.

2. In regard to the stage of a conflict, the most important issue in terms of resolution **is to address the problem early on**.

3. Since the basis for most conflicts is structural, the parties involved should be prepared to seek **clarification from someone one level above them or a specialist**.

4. In a conflict that is structurally based, it is critical that the parties involved spend time examining such issues as **clarity of roles, outcomes, expectations, sources of information, differences in evaluation or interpretation of information, and differences in perception** before they attempt any problem-solving.

5. Conflict is absolutely unavoidable; it is a **normal condition** of people actively living and working together.

6. The longer a conflict goes unaddressed and unresolved, the more **difficult** it is to resolve.

7. What makes conflict so very difficult is that it is really three separate problems masquerading as one: **the problem itself; how to address the problem; and to whom you should speak about the problem**.

8. When the basis for a conflict is structural, what makes it impossible to resolve at the level of the parties involved is that neither person is **wrong**.

Chapter Six

Traditional Communication Methods of Conflict Resolution

ONCE YOU HAVE SOME CLARITY on the structural aspects of the conflict, your next step is to determine what might be an appropriate communication method to use in confronting the conflict. There are actually five communication methods to choose from when addressing a conflict issue:

1. You can take a win-lose stance, hoping you will be the winner.
2. You can work at compromising your differences.
3. You can collaborate with the other person to find a solution acceptable to both of you.
4. You can acquiesce to the other person's view of things.
5. You can avoid the situation altogether by denying it even exists or by running away from the resolution process.

Although there are five different communication methods available for resolving conflicts, most people will choose the same one or two methods every time. Rarely will a person utilize all five. In general, the selection of methods is a combination of habit, personal reference, comfort level, and personality.

The unconscious limiting of methods creates two problems. First of all, if you always use the same method for every conflict situation, you become predictable. Your opponents will always know exactly what you are likely to do. Secondly, if you depend on habit, personal preference, comfort level, and personality as a strategy for addressing a conflict, you have denied yourself serious thought regarding which of the five methods might work best for you in a particular situation. Therefore, if you intend to become proficient at resolving conflict, you *must* be able to utilize all five methods. This is because some methods work well in some situations and are not very effective in others. What follows is a brief explanation of each of the five methods and some information about the situations in which each method is especially effective.

The attempt to reconcile a conflict can be described along two dimensions. First is the extent to which a person will attempt to satisfy his or her own needs, and second is the extent to which that same person will attempt to satisfy the concerns of his opponent.

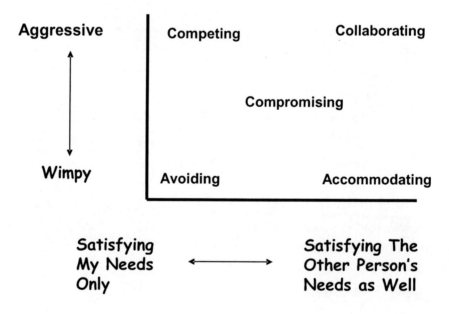

Here is a great example of what can happen when a person approaches every conflict situation in the same manner. Many years ago, I had a person named Connie working for me. She was very good at her job. Although I had tried to teach her about not always approaching every situation wearing the same battle gear, my efforts never took.

Connie and her mother had always been very close, so Connie was devastated when her mother died of a sudden heart attack. It was only then that Connie discovered her father had been suffering from Alzheimer's disease. Her mother had been concealing her father's health situation.

Now it became Connie's responsibility to look after her father, along with her own home and job responsibilities. She became bitter and angry. She was harsh with the office staff and my clients. I believed that if I waited patiently for three or four months, the old Connie would return. Her behavior, however, continued to deteriorate. Clients were complaining. Her attitude was hurting the business. I decided that I would have to let her go.

In my state, after they fire an employee, small companies must pay a continuing large unemployment tax. The tax does not apply, however, if an employee decides to quit of her own volition. It would obviously save me a considerable amount of money if I could get Connie to quit.

Knowing that Connie faced every conflict situation with a competing method, I set her up. She was due for a raise the following month. I told her that before I would consider raising her salary, I wanted her to listen to a series of audio tapes entitled "Serving Customers by Phone."

Connie:	I refuse to do that unless you pay me for the time it takes for me to listen to those stupid tapes.
Me:	I don't intend to pay you for that time. I believe you should work at becoming more proficient at your job. I don't want to give you a raise just for being here another year.
Connie:	(With her voice up several decibels) What's wrong with the way I do my job?

Me:	Nothing. It's just that we should all be working at getting better at what we do.
Connie:	Well I'm not going to listen to any damn tapes, and if you don't give me my raise on the first of next month, I will quit!

Wow, I thought, *success on the first try*. But I felt like a heel.

Me:	Connie, surely you don't mean that. Surely you're not going to quit over listening to six hours of audio tape.
Connie:	As a matter of principle, I will quit. I'm so upset about this that I'm going home right now. You can call me and leave a message on my answering machine that I don't have to listen to those tapes and that my raise will be effective beginning next Monday, or you will never see me again!

Then Connie stormed her way out of the office. I never did see Connie again. When Connie registered for her unemployment, I was able to report, quite honestly, that she had quit of her own volition. As a result, my tax rate was never increased. This outcome would never have been possible if Connie had not been so predictable in how she approached conflict situations.

The conflict-handling communication method which Connie utilized is known as *competing*. She was attempting to satisfy her own needs at the expense of her opponent's (me) needs. It is a win-lose approach which is both aggressive and uncooperative. The underlying desire is to do whatever is necessary to win.

The competing method is a practical strategy in cases where quick, decisive action is necessary, as in the case of an emergency. It is also useful where unpopular action must be implemented because it is vital to safety and welfare. It is also useful in standing up for your rights or in defending a position which you know is right. Finally, it is useful in situations where you need protection from those who would otherwise take advantage of you.

Dana had been a powerhouse in the public relations industry before her marriage. Now, after spending eighteen years as a housewife and mother to five children, she wanted to return to the workforce and restart her public relations career. When she told her family about her plans, everyone was very supportive. However, since Dana would be working full time, all the traditional household chores would now have to be maintained by her husband and kids. She suggested a weekly round-robin sharing of the tasks of shopping, cooking, cleaning, laundry, and yard work. The family happily agreed.

The very next day, she started on a six-week program to update her computer and general office knowledge. For that six-week period, all went well at home. At the end of the six weeks, her old firm happily gave Dana a job in the area where she had excelled so long ago.

After her first full day of work, all that family support for handling the household fell apart. The shopping hadn't been done, no one had prepared dinner, and the kitchen was still dirty with the remains of breakfast.

"What's going on?" Dana asked. No one had an answer. The youngest, a twelve-year-old, responded with a question.

"What's for dinner, Mom?"

"I don't know," Dana responded. "I'm eating out." With that she walked out the door.

Later that evening, her husband complained that he did not have a clean, ironed shirt to wear at his very important business meeting the next day.

"The stores are still open," Dana said. "Perhaps you should run out and purchase a new shirt."

As the week continued, her children and husband bombarded her with complaints regarding the impact on them personally of the household chores not being done. With each complaint came the unspoken expectation that it was her duty to do something about their problem.

That Sunday, Dana prepared a spectacular dinner, which included everyone's favorite dishes. She waited until all the members of her family had their mouths full of food and so could not interrupt her or argue with her.

Then Dana stood up at her place and announced: "I have spent eighteen years doing everything to make your lives comfortable. When I explained that it was now time for me to do something for myself and restart my career, you all agreed to take on the responsibility of the household chores. None of you have kept your word. This makes me very angry. Therefore, I want you all to understand that this is the last meal I will cook in this house. If you intend to eat here, wear clean clothes, and live in a clean environment, you will have to take care of those things yourselves." Dana then sat down to eat.

Her family was stunned—but evidently not enough to take her seriously. The situation at the house continued to deteriorate. Within a week, the dirty dishes in the sink were piled so high they almost reached the ceiling. Even though theirs was the third house in on the street, Dana could smell the rotting food from the corner of the block. Finally, when the last soda cracker in the cupboard had been eaten, and the last bit of peanut butter had been scraped from the jar, Dana's husband and children sat down and divided up the chores. In all, it took three weeks before her family came to their senses. Dana had used a competing method to resolve this conflict, because she felt that her family was taking advantage of her. Although she had to wait them out, Dana was determined not to let her family of capable young adults force her into the untenable position of having to maintain the house while working full time.

Now let's look at how Gary, a young supervisor of a group of older men handled his safety situation with a competing approach. Gary had been promoted to a supervisory position of a team of telephone repair linemen. These are the guys who climb up the roadside telephone poles when line repairs are necessary. Among the men at this telephone company, this particular job was considered especially dangerous, and seriously macho, since the work is done without safety harnesses. When the government mandated the use of harnesses to perform line repairs, these guys refused to comply. Their explanation was simple. The use of the safety equipment eliminated all the danger, and therefore all the machismo, from the job.

Although Gary tried to reason with his employees, his efforts were ignored. With his company's concurrence, Gary resorted to using a competing strategy. He told the guys that anyone climbing the poles without the required safety harnesses would be fired. Gary's team decided to utilize the harnesses.

Before using this method, however, it would be prudent to consider whether you will ever again need the help and cooperation of the others involved. At work and at home, a conflict may simply be a brief event in a long life of many interactions. A competing approach often creates a desire for reprisal in the loser.

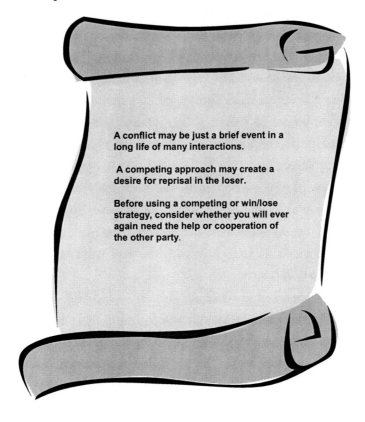

A conflict may be just a brief event in a long life of many interactions.

A competing approach may create a desire for reprisal in the loser.

Before using a competing or win/lose strategy, consider whether you will ever again need the help or cooperation of the other party.

The *collaborating* method is one in which a person attempts to satisfy both his own needs and the needs of the other person. The underlying desire is to find a solution that satisfies both parties so that, in the end, both feel like winners. The collaborating method is a useful strategy in cases where both sets of concerns are too important to be compromised. It is also useful in situations where people need a consensual decision or a strong commitment to ensure that the agreed-upon outcome will work. People also use this method to gain new perspectives and insights into seemingly intractable problems. The collaborating approach forces the parties to dig into an issue and identify or uncover all underlying factors. Negotiation attempts in foreign affairs, such as the peace efforts regarding the Middle East turmoil, are always done using the collaborating method. Here is an example of a conflict situation in which the most effective method for producing a resolution is the collaborating method.

Jim's younger brother Mike has defaulted on a car loan on which Jim is the co-signer. The bank which holds the car loan has now threatened to put a garnishment on Jim's wages, unless he brings the payments up to date. Jim is being seriously considered for a promotion at the financial services firm where he works. A garnishment will undoubtedly kill his chances for promotion and might seriously threaten his continued employment there.

Mike has been a royal pain in the neck for years. He'd been in serious trouble as a kid. As an adult, he borrows money, never pays it back, and he regularly mooches meals from Jim and his family. Whenever Jim asks Mike to help with the yard work or look after the kids, he's always too busy.

Mike dropped out of school at sixteen to run with a wild crowd. Drugs and booze came next. After spending a little time in jail, he straightened out, completed a GED, and got a sales job. Mike began to make pretty good money as an inside salesperson. Soon Mike's company offered to put him on the road. In order to accept this new, more lucrative, position, Mike would need a car. He convinced his older brother, Jim, to co-sign the car loan.

Because Mike was the newest outside salesman, he was given the worst territory. Then business slowed because of the economy. Mike believes he can make this new position a success if he gives it a little more time and a lot of effort. Meanwhile, Mike has not been able to make the last three car payments. Now the bank is threatening to repossess the car. If that happens, he will have no job at all. Mike wants Jim to assume his car payments for the next several months or until he is making sufficient income to handle the payments himself.

Since Jim has a family to support, he doesn't want the added expense of paying for someone else's car for some indefinite amount of time. On the other hand, Jim certainly doesn't want to endanger his position at the financial services company where he works. A garnishment would show his employer that he is irresponsible when it comes to managing his finances. Therefore, they would wonder if they could depend on Jim to help others manage their finances.

When Jim and Mike sat down to resolve their situation using a collaborative method, the result with which both brothers felt satisfied was quite simple. Jim agreed to pay Mike's car payments for the next six months. Mike agreed to begin repayment beginning in the seventh month. Mike also agreed to provide once a week baby sitting services free of charge plus four hours per week of yard services assistance until the loan was paid off.

The problem with collaboration is that it takes time—a lot of time—to produce results. Therefore, many people will employ the collaborating method for major issues and then switch to the compromising method for items of less importance. Labor-management negotiations in industry are set up to work this way.

The *compromising* method is both very direct and cooperative. The underlying desire is to find some expedient, mutually acceptable solution that will partially satisfy both parties. It is a temporary solution, usually arrived at by each party giving up something he or she wants in order to arrive at a middle ground. Compromising is about splitting the difference in order to move on. The compromising method is useful in situations where the individual goals of the parties involved are moderately important but not worth the effort of a long, drawn-out collaboration. Compromising is also useful in obtaining a temporary settlement to a complex issue or to arrive at an expedient solution when both parties are under time pressure. Finally, it is a great method to use when the parties involved have equal power organizationally and are both strongly committed to mutually exclusive goals.

Here is an example of a situation in which a compromising method would be most appropriate in solving the problem. Let's suppose that you have a next-door neighbor who owns a huge dog. The dog thinks your well-cared-for, manicured yard is the perfect place for him to do his business, bury his bones, and make urine patches on your lawn. You have asked your neighbor to tie up his dog so that he cannot get into your yard. Your neighbor believes that his dog needs a reasonable amount of freedom to move around. Being chained up would not only limit his mobility, it would make him very unhappy. He suggests you fence your property. You do not want to fence your property.

You approach your neighbor with a somewhat costly solution. You suggest that if he put up an electronic fence, you will assist him with the cost. The neighbor now realizes just how much his dog is aggravating you. He also is surprised at your very reasonable offer to help with the cost of fencing in his property, when the two of you just share one side of the land. He tells you that if you will consider paying 20 percent of the total cost, he will go ahead with putting in an electronic fence. Since you'd thought he might ask you for 50 percent of the cost, you jump at this deal.

The *avoiding* method is both antisocial and uncooperative. The underlying desire is to avoid pursuing one's own concerns or the concerns of the other party. In fact, this is a strategy of not addressing the conflict at all—of diplomatically side-stepping the issues. The avoiding method is useful when the conflict is trivial or of minor importance. It is also a great tool when other issues are more pressing.

When political figures are interviewed by the news media, they generally use an avoiding method. Perhaps this is because they wish to steer clear of making any portion of their constituency unhappy over whatever their true stance on a particular issue might be.

Newsperson: Senator Jones, how do you intend to vote on the measure now before Congress?

Senator Jones: Well, this is a very important issue which will impact every American.

Newsperson: Certainly our viewers understand that, Senator Jones. So, how do you intend to vote on this critical measure?

Senator Jones: My colleagues and I have been in serious discussion over this issue for several weeks now. I assure you we do not take this responsibility lightly.

Newsperson: The vote is scheduled to take place tomorrow. How do you intend to vote the measure?

Senator Jones: We have reached across party lines to ensure that all sides of the issue have been explored. The American People expect that, and we will not let them down.

Newsperson: As always, your candor and honesty are appreciated.

Senator Jones: Thank you. Good to be with you.

Avoiding is a practical method in situations where people are emotional and need time to cool down before productive discussions can take place. Sometimes a person might just be having a bad day. You use an avoiding method today, and the next day the person tells you, "I don't know what got into me yesterday. I apologize if I said anything that upset you." Avoiding is an essential tactic when gathering additional information is critical to a good decision. The avoiding method is frequently used when an employee or child complains about something to a manager or parent, who responds, "Let me look into it. When I have more information, we can talk about this again."

Finally, the avoiding method is a good choice when you perceive that you have no chance of satisfying your own concerns, because of your lack of organizational power, or because the situation would be impossible to change no matter what happened. In other words, "He who runs away lives to fight another day."

The *accommodating* or *acquiescing* method is unassertive and cooperative. The underlying desire is to neglect one's own concerns while fully satisfying the concerns of the other person. With this method, there is an element of self-sacrifice and selfless generosity—giving in to another person even though you would prefer not to do so. Often it is used as a goodwill gesture to ensure a continuing cooperative relationship. Sometimes people use it to prove they are reasonable. Accommodating is an effective method when the issue in question is very important to one person but of trivial concern to the other. Often the accommodating method is used to build up "credits," which can be cashed in later on issues of greater importance. When this is going on, you will hear such remarks as, "Okay, I'll support you on this one, but you owe me."

Accommodating is a great tool to use when, in the midst of a conflict, you realize you are wrong. Instead of saying, "Sorry, I guess I was wrong," you might say, "Well, Sarah, if it's that important to you, we'll do it your way." Sometimes in a conflict, a person realizes that continued confrontation will only hurt her cause, perhaps because she is outmatched or is losing badly. At such times an accommodating method is a graceful way of bowing out. Finally, the accommodating method is useful when you want someone to learn from his or her own mistakes. Parents make use of this one when they say to a child, "All right! Do what you want! You'll learn the hard way!"

Methods of Conflict-Handling

Methods	Goal of the Method	Works Best in Situations Where ...	Problems and Cautions
Compete or win/lose	win at any cost	emergencies; quick decisive action is needed; standing up for your rights;	creates a desire for reprisal in the loser
Collaborate or teamwork	win-win	both sets of concerns are very important; need a strong commitment to successfully implement the outcome; to dig into an issue and uncover all the factors	takes time; lots of time to produce results
Compromise or bargaining	negotiate the difference	parties are under time pressure; goals of the parties are moderately important; to arrive at a temporary, expedient solution which partially satisfy both people; both parties involved have equal power organizationally and are committed to mutually exclusive goals	provides short-tem, temporary solutions; bargaining may create a gamesmanship climate
Avoid or dodging	avoidance	the conflict is trivial or of minor importance; when other issues are more pressing; people are emotional and need time to cool down; gathering additional information is critical; you have no chance of satisfying your concerns	decisions important to you are made by default; avoiding issues that need to be faced create anxiety depression
Accommodate or giving in	preserve harmony	the issue in question is trivial to you but very important to the other; used to ensure goodwill and a cooperative relationship; to prove you are reasonable; to accumulate "credits"; when you realize you're wrong; to preserve peace; to let someone "learn from their own mistakes"	your own concerns may not get the attention they need; helpful if you have difficulty admitting when you're wrong;

So, as you can see, there are five different methods available to you for approaching a conflict. Of the five, you probably have a favorite, which you use most of the time, and one other which you use as a back-up method when your favorite isn't producing results. To be truly effective at resolving conflict, however, you must be able to use all five methods. As in everything else, including clothing, one size does not fit all.

Let's revisit the irresponsible brother-in-law loan situation. Suppose you decide to use the competing, or win-lose, method. You say to your brother-in-law, "If you don't repay the loan by the first of next month, I will sue you." The brother-in-law can't pay the loan by that time, and so you take him to court. This really pleases your spouse (not!), who gives you plenty of grief over the situation. Moreover, the judge in the case is sympathetic to your brother-in-law and orders him to repay you at the rate of $50 per month. It will take more than sixteen years for you to recover the borrowed funds.

Suppose you decide to use the compromising method (let's split the difference between what I want – full payment - and what you can afford to pay) with your brother-in-law. You say to him, "I'd really appreciate it if you could start repaying the loan. What might you be comfortable with on a per-month basis?" Since you sound reasonable, the brother-in-law reciprocates and says, "I think I could manage $500 a month. More than that would be quite a stretch for me." At $500 per month, the loan would be repaid in just under two years. You'd really like this loan to be repaid in full within the next twelve months, so you say, "If you can see your way clear to pay $850 per month, the loan would be paid off in about one year. That would work well for me. What do you say?" The brother-in-law thinks for a moment and then responds, "I understand where you're coming from, but $850 is too steep for me. How about we split the difference at $675 per month?" That figure gets the loan repaid in fifteen months. You feel that's a good compromise, so you agree.

If you were to utilize the avoidance method, you might decide never to mention the loan at all and hope that some day in the distant future your brother-in-law will pay back the loan. This means, however, that you have to accept the fact that the brother-in-law received a ten-thousand-dollar gift from you. If you are not willing to forgive the loan, then you should not choose an avoidance strategy. The reason is that your hostility around being taken advantage of may not go away. Instead, your hostility might seep into the relationship and eventually destroy it.

Forgiving the loan would represent the accommodating method. In this case, you would tell your brother-in-law of your decision in a straightforward manner, such as: "Gladys and I have decided that our loan to you of ten thousand dollars should be considered a gift. Therefore, you do not have to repay us."

It would *not* be appropriate to say something like: "Since Gladys and I recognize you're a complete asshole when it comes to money, and that we don't stand a chance in hell of getting you to repay it, we have decided to regard that ten-thousand-dollar loan as a gift."

Once you become aware of how you and other people utilize the various conflict-approaching methods, you recognize that in order for you to successfully utilize the compromising or collaborating method, the other party must utilize a similar strategy. Suppose, for example, that you approach the loan situation with a desire to compromise (on a sum of monthly repayments), but your brother-in-law utilizes a competing or win-lose method (to achieve not paying you anything).

You: I'd really appreciate it if you could start repaying the loan. What might you be comfortable with on a per-month basis?

Bro: What do you mean, repayment? I'm sure you don't need the money. Besides, you know how tough things are for me right now. I'll thank you not to add to my already considerable stress.

Suppose your brother-in-law decides to use an avoidance method cleverly masked as the accommodation method.

You: I'd really appreciate it if you could start repaying the loan. What might you be comfortable with on a per-month basis?

Bro: Right. Absolutely. I plan to start repaying you right away. Don't worry. I'll send you something next week or maybe by the end of the month.

There has to be a way for you to modify another person's conflict-handling method so that the two of you can engage in a successful problem-solving conversation. To do that, you must stand up, so that you and your adversary are physically level. Keep your hands at your sides. Speak in a non-threatening, but very firm, voice. State your purpose or goal clearly (to get some kind of agreement regarding the repayment of the loan). Then ask an open-ended question, which begins with the words

what
   when
      where
         who
            how
               why (Use *why* very, very sparingly.)

You: I would like us to agree on a formal payment schedule. What might you be comfortable with on a per-month basis?

Bro: Oh, we don't need a formal schedule. Believe me. I have every intention of paying you back, just as soon as I get caught up on some things.

You:	I understand. However, I would like us to agree on a formal payment schedule. When would it be convenient for you to make the first payment?
Bro:	Well, I really can't say. Ummmm—can't you just trust me?
You:	Of course. But I'd still like us to agree on a formal payment schedule. How do you feel about $550 per month with the first payment being today?
Bro:	Today? Not today. It's almost the end of the month. I'm totally out of funds.
You:	Then, when would it be convenient for you to make the first payment?

Let's look at another example. Suppose you work for a boss who has a short fuse. Giving him any bad news, such as a delay on the completion of a project, will absolutely result in getting your head blown off. As team leader on the project, however, it is your responsibility to report on the status of the project to the department manager, Hollering Harry Holman. You prepare for the meeting by writing out a list of the reasons why the project will be late. You also examine the communication methods available to you and select the accommodating method (accommodating his hostility without getting caught up in it), because

1. It is a sure thing that Hollering Harry will use a competing method.
2. His yelling will compel you into a defensive posture, which you want to avoid.
3. In order to negotiate a resolution, you have to force Hollering Harry into a method other than his usual aggressive, competing method.

After your initial statement informing Hollering Harry that the project will be late, you step back and await the verbal onslaught that is sure to follow. It does. You then hand Hollering Harry your written list of reasons why the project is late, and you ask, "What do you think should be done now to rectify the situation?" (There is more information on this method of altering another person's method of addressing conflict in Chapter 14.)

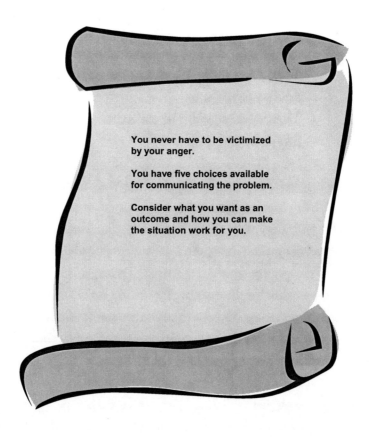

You never have to be victimized by your anger.

You have five choices available for communicating the problem.

Consider what you want as an outcome and how you can make the situation work for you.

Now, you are probably thinking, "How am I supposed to stop and consider which method would have the best chance for success in a particular situation when I am so angry I can't even see straight?"

Conventional wisdom tells us that no matter how angry we might be, it is always better not to speak out in the heat of the moment. We might say or do things we will ultimately regret. We all know that. The problem with the strategy of not speaking out in the heat of the moment is that it is a lot easier in concept than it is in practice. The next chapter will show you how to take a mental *time-out* to plan a strategy for your response. Then you will go back later and revisit the conflict situation with your adversary. In this way, you will be able to handle any conflict situation with confidence and competence.

Chapter Six Exercises

Directions: The following statements represent a simple review of what you have just learned regarding the methods for conflict resolution.

1. A person using a competing or win-lose method for conflict resolution
   - is basically a bully
   - had better have no need for the cooperation of the other person ever again
   - is pursuing his own interests at the expense of the other party
   - is standing up for his rights which he feels have been ignored
   - believes he is are 100 percent right and the other side is 100 percent wrong
   - has become inflexible in his position
   - all of the above
2. A person using an avoid-conflict-at-all-costs method
   - is basically a wuss: impotent, weak, and inept
   - believes that he who runs away lives to fight another day
   - has decided the issue is trivial and not worth a problem-solving effort
   - is a diplomat who knows how to sidestep troublesome issues
   - is unassertive, uninvolved, and uncooperative
   - may be just putting off a discussion until a better time
   - may be apathetic—she doesn't care what the outcome is
   - all of the above

3. A person using a compromising method for conflict resolution
   - believes in splitting the difference
   - seeks a resolution that partially satisfies both parties
   - gives a little to get a little
   - is interested in expedient and timely resolutions
   - never really gets 100 percent of what she wants
   - avoids exploring the conflict in depth, ensuring it will reoccur
   - all of the above

4. Identify which of the items below is *not* true: Conflict is an absolute certainty when you
   - act on assumptions rather than facts
   - expect more from others than they are willing or able to give
   - are not clear with yourself and others about your basic values
   - feel apathetic and uninvolved
   - make promises that are not kept
   - try to change someone else
   - criticize others openly or subtly with snide jokes or telling looks

5. You bring a conflict issue to your boss. She tells you to handle the situation yourself. What is she actually telling you?
   - your problem is too trivial for me to get involved with
   - you can handle that issue much more effectively than I can
   - you should ask questions; make sure I will support your decisions
   - don't be such a wimp; go fight your own battles
   - I will support whatever resolution you and the other person choose
   - all of the above

6. You and another person are attempting to resolve a conflict. The other person is using the collaborative method. You should therefore use the _____ method.

7. Events have put you in a very angry frame of mind. You are due to have an important discussion with your boss in thirty minutes. Your wisest strategy is to _____ that meeting.

8. A co-worker has been taking advantage of you. You want to confront him about it. You should use the _____ method.

9. The most important thing to do before going into a conflict-resolving discussion is to _____.

10. In a conflict-resolving discussion, if you are willing to split the difference, you should use a _____ method.

11. If you continually use an avoid-conflict-at-all-costs strategy, you will probably never _____.

12. For you, the conflict issue is trivial; for the other person, it is critical. This is the ideal situation for you to utilize a _____ resolution method and build up some goodwill.

13. Acts of reprisal are usually the result of one party using a _____ method to solve a problem.

14. You and a co-worker are in a conflict over something that both of you recognize is trivial. Your most effective conflict resolution method is _____.

15. You are in a conflict- resolving discussion in which the other person seems anxious to find a quick Band-Aid or expedient solution. The other person is using the _____ method of conflict resolution.

Answers to Chapter Six Exercises

1. A person using a win-lose strategy for conflict resolution ... Every item listed in this question is true, so the answer is **all of the above**. Like all strategies for conflict resolution, there are instances where using a win-lose approach is appropriate.

2. A person using an avoid-conflict-at-all-costs strategy ... The answer here is **all of the above**. Some of the items shown are valid, such as putting off discussion until a better time, or believing that the issue is too trivial to deal with. Other reasons, such as being a wuss, or feeling impotent, weak, and inept or unassertive, uninvolved and uncooperative are not valid. It may not be your style to confront people about your dissatisfactions, but once in a while, especially if your character or dignity has been impugned, it's a good idea to step out of your comfort zone, confront your adversary, and regain the respect you deserve. Otherwise, you go through life feeling like a pawn in someone else's game.

3. A person using a compromising strategy for conflict resolution ... The correct response here is **all of the above**. This is probably the most popular strategy in conflict resolution, because it offers a quick result. Most people today are so busy that there is simply no time to engage in an excavation of the problem. All they want is enough of a resolution so that they can move on.

   Since things are constantly changing, when the problem reappears at some point in the future, the situation may look quite different and, therefore, so will the preferred strategy for its resolution. However, the parties will have experienced a conflict-resolving success. They will have the confidence that they can do it again, probably with less effort and anxiety.

4. Conflict is an absolute certainty … The answer here is **when you feel apathetic and uninvolved.** All the other items listed are certain to generate conflict. Sometimes it appears as if a particular person is always in a state of conflict with co-workers, their boss, or a family member. Just as some people are accident-prone, this person is conflict-prone. Most likely, the reason is their typical behavior pattern revolves around one or more of the items listed in this question.

5. If you bring a conflict problem to your boss and he/she tells you … The correct response is **all of the above.** However, behind every one of the choices listed is the unspoken guarantee that your boss will support whatever resolution you and the other person choose. A good strategy would be to ask a few additional questions to ensure that he will indeed support your decision.

   Bosses, in general, hate to get themselves involved in resolving their staff's conflicts. What works well is to describe the conflict issue to your boss and then tell him how you intend to deal with it. You may get some additional problem-solving ideas. Most of all, you'll get your boss's support for your effort and your chosen solution.

   There is an additional issue you might keep in mind. When people are interviewed for very senior, top level positions, one of the things they are inevitably asked about is their ability to manage conflict without utilizing outside resources. You give yourself a career boost when you show that you are able to resolve conflicts on your own.

6. The other person is using a collaborative strategy to resolve a conflict with you. You should therefore use a **collaborative** method.

7. Events have put you in a very angry state of mind. You are due to have an important discussion with your boss in thirty minutes. Your wisest strategy is to **avoid or postpone** that discussion.

8. A co-worker has been taking advantage of you. You want to confront her about it. You should use a **competing** method.

9. The most important thing to do before going into a conflict-resolving discussion is **to plan a strategy including a communication method.**

10. In a conflict-resolving discussion, if you are willing to split the difference you should use a **compromising** method.

11. If you continually use an avoid-conflict-at-all-costs strategy, you will probably never get **your needs met or your problems solved.**

12. For you, the conflict issue is trivial; for the other person, it is critical. This is the ideal situation for you to utilize **an accommodating method** and build up some goodwill.

13. Acts of reprisal are usually the result of one party using a **competing** method to solve a problem.

14. You and a co-worker are in a conflict over something both of you recognizes is trivial. Your best conflict resolution method is to **compromise.**

15. You are in a conflict-resolving discussion in which the other person seems anxious to find a quick Band-Aid or expedient solution. The other person is using the **compromise method** of conflict resolution.

Chapter Seven

Addressing the Conflict: The Assertive Script

WHEN YOU PREPARE TO CONFRONT another person about something that is aggravating you, it is important to use an *assertive* approach. An assertive approach is one that endeavors to accomplish two things:

- to achieve a specific result or resolve a particular problem
- to avoid disrespect to the other person in the process.

The assertive approach seeks a win-win outcome. It recognizes there is a continuing interdependent relationship, and therefore there will be future opportunities for interaction.

An *aggressive* approach also seeks to accomplish two things:

- to achieve a specific result at any cost
- to extract an emotional price from the other person by insulting them or putting them down in some way.

If you take an aggressive stance, you are pursuing a win-lose outcome. If that is what you want, be absolutely certain that you will never again need the other person's help or cooperation. In a win-lose outcome, the loser will be looking for an opportunity to *get even*. As the saying goes, "What goes around comes around."

A *nonassertive* response also seeks to accomplish two things:

- to avoid confrontation at all costs, even if it means sacrificing whatever one wants
- to retain the other person's positive regard

Here is an illustration of the differences between the three approaches. One of your co-workers always catches you just as you are leaving for coffee break and asks if you would pick up a coffee and donut for her while you are getting yours. It's not a big deal; it only amounts to a few bucks. However, it's been going on for many months. Not once has this person offered to pay for her own treat, nor has she ever volunteered to pay for yours. You are really aggravated at being taken advantage of in this manner.

The assertive approach: "Mel, I no longer wish to purchase coffee and donuts for you. Please don't ask me to do it any more."

The aggressive approach: "You really have one heck of a nerve expecting other people to pay for your coffee break goodies. I'm tired of being panhandled. Go get your own, you creep."

The nonassertive approach: "Gee whiz, Mel. Umm ... I'm sorry, but ... I'm kinda on a diet and ... umm, I'm not sure I can leave my work right now. You know how it is ... ahhh, I have this report to complete by the end of the day. I'm probably not going to take a break at all today. I'll get you tomorrow. Okay?"

Confronting another person about something that's been annoying you should never be done on the spur of the moment. Effective confrontation requires thought, careful preparation, and practice. This is because your own stress can get in the way, especially if you have been fuming about a situation for a period of time. When stress takes over, you may say things you will later regret. Even worse, you may describe the problem with such intensity and emotionality that little room remains for discussion.

Here is an illustration of stress creating a situation where, because the person is responding without preparation, he says things that will not help resolve the problem. Moreover, after the outburst, there is no room for discussion.

Jeff has the best computer skills in the department. Jeff's boss, Evelyn, in a desire to increase her "credits" with managers in other areas, often volunteers his services to assist others with their computer problems. The difficulty is, she does this without asking if Jeff has the time and without consideration for his work priorities. Although her actions anger Jeff, to date he has said nothing. Then, in a performance feedback discussion, Evelyn tells Jeff that she is giving him an unsatisfactory mark on his evaluation, because he seems to be unable to manage his workload effectively.

In anger, Jeff blasts forth, "Goddammit to hell! How dare you tell me that! You're always dragging me away from my work to slog around solving problems in other departments. You never ask if I have the time. You never ask if I'm willing. And you never even consider how it will affect my work priorities. And now you want me to pay the price for your need to curry favor with every management person in the building. You need a psychiatrist, and I need a new boss. I want a transfer!"

After such a righteous outburst, how could Jeff ever repair that relationship? He couldn't. He might even be forced to leave the job—even though he was absolutely correct about everything he said. So, before you confront someone or speak out in anger at the moment, take the time to prepare. Then go revisit the situation with the person involved, utilizing a carefully crafted script.

Scripting   Format

Describe the situation	**when & how often**
Express how you feel **(...*that made me feel*...)**	**don't hide behind 3rd parties** **don't put yourself *down***
Specify the behavior **(...*I want you to* ...)**	**one item per script** **be specific; use numbers** **ask for behavior changes** **not attitude changes**
Question	**not answerable by *yes* or *no***

Developing an Assertive Script

The *assertive script* is a twenty-second, four-line, prepared speech that puts your concerns on the table in a clear, brief, unemotional, and professional manner. It ends in a question that invites the other person to assist in resolving the issue. For example, Jeff might say: "At least twice each week, you volunteer my computer expertise to assist people in other departments with their problems. However, you never check with me first to see how this will affect my work priorities. It makes me feel angry that you force me to utilize my time in other departments, and now you want to give me an unsatisfactory grade on my evaluation because my own workload is not being handled effectively. I want you to stop volunteering me to other departments, so that I can spend my time managing my own workload. How will you revise my evaluation to reflect this situation?"

The steps to constructing an effective script are as follows.

1. Write down exactly what you wish to say. Make it as brief as possible.
2. Explain how you feel about the situation

3. State clearly what you want as an outcome of the confrontation discussion.
4. Close with an open-ended question that solicits a problem-solving response from your adversary
5. Edit your script to four sentences that can be spoken in twenty seconds or less.

As you edit, substitute any caustic, insulting, or subjective terms that are likely to anger your opponent into tuning you out. Finally, practice your script until your stress level feels manageable. If possible, role-play your script with a friend to see how it works. Practice until your script—especially the statement of what you want (the third line)—is committed to memory. In addition, if appropriate, prepare any documentation that will support what you are going to say. Here is another example addressing a common employee-manager problem.

Describe: Boss, last week you told me I was not ready yet to take on a management role.

Express: This made me feel confused, because I am already handling many management functions in my present job.

Specify: I would appreciate it if you would provide me with a more definitive description of the skills and experience you think I am missing.

Question: What exactly am I missing?

This verbal strategy is also very effective in dealing with problems at home between parents and children and between spouses.

Describe: Alice, I have asked you three times in the past 30 minutes to turn off your computer and go to bed.

Express: I am troubled and concerned that you will be too tired in the morning to go to school and give your presentation.

Specify: I want you to turn off your computer immediately and go to bed.

Question: How embarrassed will you be if, because you are tired, your presentation turns out badly?

It is common in such confrontation-discussions for your adversary to attempt to distract you away from the topic by utilizing a variety of predictable manipulative tactics. Having your script written down, well rehearsed, and memorized will prevent you from being derailed away from the topic. Remember that you are asking for a behavior change; you are not trying to win an intellectual debate. However, you do want to be prepared.

Your goal is to negotiate for a behavior change.

It is not to win an intellectual debate.

Here are some of the manipulative methods you can expect from your adversary:

1. Changing the topic to something closely related to your issue
2. Denying the problem outright
3. Delaying the discussion and putting you off
4. Leveling a harsh, personal criticism at you
5. Claiming that you should have mentioned this before
6. Tying two unrelated things together in the form of a criticism
7. Telling you that, because of friendship, you should be more tolerant of errant behavior
8. Declaring the issue is trivial and you shouldn't concern yourself with petty issues
9. Stating that others do the exact same thing.
10. Declaring "you are the only person (in the universe?) who feels that way!"
11. Misunderstanding the message
12. Asking questions which, if answered, will lead to off-topic discussions

As the above examples illustrate, the first line in your script is known as the *describe line*. Here, you want to depict the problem situation in one sentence. It helps to state when or how often the situation has occurred. For example: "Howard, last Thursday morning when I was talking to you about the budget overrun in your area, you turned your back on me and walked away."

The next line in your script is called the *express line*, because it is here that you tell your adversary about your personal feelings regarding the situation. It begins with the words, "That made me feel _____ (however it makes you feel), because _____." It's important not to denigrate yourself in this line by saying such things as "That made me feel *stupid* because …" You will sound much stronger if you say, "That made me feel *angry* because …"

In addition, never hide behind amorphous third parties. For example, saying something like, "That made me feel angry because refusing to resolve problems makes everyone's work harder" sounds as if you are trying to remove yourself from the issue or attach the impact of the problem onto someone else, whom your adversary cannot specifically identify. What you should say is, "That made me feel angry because refusing to discuss your budget overrun makes my work harder." Make it personal, so that it becomes more difficult for your adversary to escape from having an honest discussion.

You could also say, "That made me feel angry, because your action was very disrespectful." Although that statement is true, it is also subjective. Stick to the cold, undeniable facts, which are that, by walking away, your adversary effectively ended the conversation before problem-solving could take place.

The third line in the script is called the *specify line*. It is here that you state clearly and specifically what it is that you want as an outcome of the confrontation. In fact, this line begins with the words, "I want you to ..." or "I would appreciate it if you would ..." This is the most important line of the script—because it is what the script is about.

In stating what you want, use numbers, dates, or time for specificity. For example, rather than saying, "I want us to discuss and resolve your budget overrun situation as soon as possible," it would be more effective to say, "I want us to discuss and resolve the budget overrun situation before 3:00 PM this coming Friday."

Often you will find that you have several aggravating issues with the person you wish to confront. Do not attempt to put all your issues into one specify line. Pick the one problem that is annoying you the most, and script on that single issue. Save the other topics for another time. Overloading your adversary with several issues at the same time makes your quest for resolution seem impossible. A laundry list of problems will create the impression that the situation is hopeless and no amount of talking will resolve anything.

To illustrate, let's look in on a pre-divorce couple:

She:	Why must you always slam the door when you come into the house? This is not a barn.
He:	Don't start with me. I've had a really hard day.
She:	You're not the only one who's had a hard day, you know. My job is extremely stressful every day.
He:	You have a choice. You don't have to work. You could stay home.
She:	Stay home? We could never manage on your measly salary.
He:	If you wouldn't spend so much money on clothes, makeup, and other unnecessary extravagances, we'd make out just fine.
She:	Oh yeah? What about all the money you spent on those new golf clubs? And how many times have you actually used them? Twice. Don't you dare talk to me about unnecessary extravagances!
He:	I swear to God, you're beginning to sound just like your mother.
She:	*My mother!*
He:	She belittles me every time she can, and now you're doing the same thing.
She:	And what about *your* mother? Nothing I ever do is good enough; my cooking is pathetic; my house-keeping is crummy; my—
He:	Well, she's certainly right about that. This house is a mess. It's always a mess.
She:	That's because one person can't do it all, and you're never willing to help. You can't even put your dirty clothes in the hamper. You leave them all over the bathroom and bedroom floors in little piles.

Finally, ask for behavior changes, not attitude changes. People find it fundamentally impossible to change their attitude. Asking them to do so will only frustrate them. Rather, ask for them to change their actions. For example, instead of saying, "I want you to show a more receptive attitude when I come to your office to discuss your department's budget issues." Try saying, "I want you to stop sighing and rolling your eyes skyward when I come into your office to discuss your department's budget issues."

The last line in the script is an open-ended *question*. The purpose of the question is to invite the other person to tell you what they want or how they would like to see the situation resolved. Questions for this line should begin with *what, when, where, who,* and *how*.

Refrain from asking *why* questions, because those tend to be manipulative and critical. They will only provide low-quality results. For example, "Why didn't you keep your expenditures within budget guidelines?" really means, "You incompetent, irresponsible moron; you should have kept your expenditures within budget guidelines." Such a question will likely get you an angry response and will certainly not forward the problem-solving process.

Here is how a proper script might sound:

Describe:	Howard, last Thursday morning when I was talking to you about the budget overrun in your area, you turned your back on me and walked away.
Express:	That made me feel angry, because refusing to discuss your budget overrun makes my work harder.
Specify:	I want us to discuss and resolve the budget overrun situation before 3:00 PM this coming Friday.
Question:	What would be a convenient time for us to meet for this discussion?

Let us suppose that Howard attempts to weasel his way out of having this conversation with you. Here, with the various manipulative strategies identified, is how the conversation might go:

How: I'm glad you stopped by. I wanted to ask you why you didn't approve my travel expenses for last month. *(Change of topic)*

You: We can speak about your travel expenses at some other time. Right now, I want us to discuss and resolve the budget overrun situation before 3:00 PM this coming Friday.

How: I am certain that I did not run over my budget. *(Outright denial)*

You: I'm afraid you did, and that's why I want us to discuss and resolve the budget overrun situation before 3:00 PM this coming Friday.

How: This week is a very busy time; it's the end of the quarter, and I've got a ton of work to do. Why don't we schedule a meeting for sometime next month? *(Delaying)*

You: The end of the quarter is precisely why we need to resolve this problem now, and that's why I want us to discuss and resolve the budget overrun situation before 3:00 PM this coming Friday.

How: Nobody around here appreciates your penny-pinching attitude. After all, it's not your money. It wouldn't hurt you to be a little less anal to the rest of us who are actually responsible for the company's income. *(Harsh, personal criticism)*

You: We are not discussing how others regard the way I do my job. We are talking about the problem of your budget overrun, and I want us to discuss and resolve the budget overrun situation before 3:00 PM this coming Friday.

How:	When you first became aware that I had gone over my budget, you should have talked to me about it then. Instead, you waited until the end of the quarter, when I'm at my busiest. Do you think that's fair? (*You should have mentioned this before.*)
You:	Well, I'm talking to you about it *now*, and I want us to discuss and resolve the budget overrun situation before 3:00 PM this coming Friday.
How:	If you were really interested in seeing this company prosper, you wouldn't be so compulsive about a little budget lapse. (*Tie two unrelated things together*)
You:	It isn't a little budget lapse; it's a matter of twenty-eight thousand dollars, and I want us to discuss and resolve the budget overrun situation before 3:00 PM this coming Friday.
How:	Look, we've known one another for a long time. We've both worked hard to help this company grow. You should realize that I wouldn't be spending company funds without a very good reason. (*Friendship equals tolerance for errant behavior*)
You:	That's why I want us to discuss and resolve the budget overrun situation before 3:00 PM this coming Friday.
How:	This is such a trivial matter, hardly worth your time. My budget issues are not a big deal. You should be worrying about important stuff, like the new tax laws. (*This is a trivial matter and not worth your concern*)
You:	Monitoring departmental budgets is a crucial part of my responsibilities, and that's why I want us to discuss and resolve the budget overrun situation before 3:00 PM this coming Friday.

How: I'm not the only manager around here that runs over his budget now and then. I know for a fact that Angela is way over budget and I don't see you talking to her. (*Others do the exact same thing*)

You: Never mind about Angela. Right now I'm speaking with *you* about *your* budget issues, and I want us to discuss and resolve your budget overrun situation before 3:00 PM this coming Friday.

How: Are you upset because I purchased advanced software for my people and didn't clear it with you first, or is it because I gave my staff half a day off last Friday? (*Asking questions that, if answered, will lead to off-topic discussions*)

You: We can discuss your purchases and the management of your staff at some later date. Right now I want us to discuss and resolve your budget overrun situation before 3:00 PM this coming Friday.

How: Fred, my previous boss, never said anything to me about the importance of strictly keeping within budget guidelines. Everyone around here knows that our budget numbers are only guidelines. You must be the only person around here that thinks budget numbers are etched in stone. (*You are the only person in the world who feels that way*)

You: I am not concerned with how others feel about their budget numbers. My concern is with your twenty-eight thousand dollars over-budget, unsubstantiated expenditures this quarter. That's why I want us to discuss and resolve the budget overrun situation before 3:00 PM this coming Friday.

How:	Are you telling me that I have to obtain written approval before I make any expenditures? (*Misunderstanding the message*)
You:	No. I'm not saying that. What I am saying is I want us to discuss and resolve the budget overrun situation before 3:00 PM this coming Friday.
How:	My God! You're like a dog with a bone. Okay. Let's meet tomorrow first thing, and I'll explain everything.
You:	First thing? I'll be in your office at 8:30 tomorrow morning.
How:	Let's make that 9:00 AM. I need to make a few important phone calls first.
You:	Okay. Then 9:00 AM it is.

Why Do I Have To Repeat Myself?

Others Do Not Hear What We Say Because They...

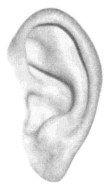

- are thinking up a response.
- are a *selective listener* – hearing only what they want to hear.
- think they already know what we are going to say.
- really don't care what we have to say.
- do not want to hear what we have to say.
- are mentally occupied by other concerns.
- have heard it all before.
- are distracted.
- have tuned us out.
- are on a mental trip.
- do not like us.

It seems impossible that a person would be able to come up with such a long series of manipulations in order to avoid having a conversation. In fact, most people will only come up with three or four avoidance tactics before finally acquiescing to your request to begin problem-solving. The continuing repetition of the *specify line* is what keeps the conversation on target. The technique is known as *the broken record*. This strategy will be discussed more fully further on in the book.

Suppose the problem concerned you and your teenager who had come home from a party at a time much later than you both had agreed upon.

Describe:	Ken, yesterday we agreed that you would be home from Emily's party by 1:00 AM. However you did not walk in the door until 2:30 AM.
Express:	This makes me feel angry and used, because I trusted you to keep your word and you did not.
Specify:	I want you to tell me how I can trust you to keep your word about anything.
Question:	How can I trust you?

Ken:	Aw, gee whiz, Mom. It's not a big deal. I was just a little late, that's all.
You:	Ninety minutes is a very big deal. I want you to tell me how I can trust you to keep your word about anything in the future.
Ken:	The party was in full swing at 1:00 AM. Nobody was leaving yet.
You:	That is not an acceptable reason for not keeping your word. You promised me that you would be home by 1:00 AM, and you were not. I want you to tell me how I can ever trust you to keep your word about anything in the future.
Ken:	That's not fair, Mom. I'm sure other parents would be much more understanding.

You:	My understanding is not the issue here. The issue is about you keeping your word. I want you to tell me how I can ever trust you to keep your word about anything in the future.
Ken:	The party was just down the block. Emily's parents were there. No liquor was being served. So, what's the big deal?
You:	The big deal is you did not keep your word. You proved that I cannot trust you. I want you to tell me how I can believe anything you promise in the future.
Ken:	Are you upset because you waited up for me to get home? You didn't have to do that, you know. I can take care of myself.
You:	My waiting up is not the issue. The issue is your inability to keep your word. I want you to tell me how I can trust you to keep your word about anything in the future.
Ken:	If I had called you and explained that the party was really getting hot and that no one was going to leave until much later and asked permission to stay longer, would that have been acceptable?
You:	Yes. I want you to tell me how I can trust you to keep your word about anything in the future.
Ken:	I guess I didn't realize that keeping my word was so important.
You:	Well, it is. This is about trust. I want you to tell me how I can trust you in the future.
Ken:	Just give me another chance. I do want you to trust that I can keep my word.

Chapter Seven Exercises

Directions: In the following problem situations, please rewrite the scripts so that each one follows this blueprint.

1. State the problem clearly, utilizing specific data.
2. Avoid subjective terms or disparaging words.
3. Declare how you feel without denigrating yourself.
4. Refrain from hiding behind amorphous third parties.
5. Announce clearly what you want as an outcome of the discussion.
6. Address only one issue or problem.
7. End with an open-ended question that encourages problem-solving.

The recommended rewrites will be found following the exercises.

Script One

Describe: Rosemary, there are many times when I ask for your assistance, and, although you are not busy, you get really huffy and nasty and refuse to help me.

Express: This is not good for our family's team effort at the household chores, and everyone suffers because of your lack of cooperation.

Specify: I want you to realize what your rotten attitude and lack of team spirit is doing.

Question: How come you are always so inconsiderate of others?

_____

_____

_____

_____

_____

Script Two

Describe: Jerry, you are the most inconsiderate person I know when it comes to taking lunch breaks.

Express: You lateness aggravates all of us, because we have to shorten our lunch breaks to accommodate you.

Specify: Get yourself a watch and stay away from the new car showrooms during lunch time.

Question: Don't you understand that your thoughtless actions affect the entire staff?

_____

_____

_____

_____

_____

Script Three

Describe: Alicia, I must have asked you seventy-five thousand times not to hum while we're working together.

Express: I find it very aggravating that you're still doing it, even though you know it kills my concentration.

Specify: I would appreciate it if you would not do a sing-along while we're working together.

Question: Is that too much to ask?

_____

_____

_____

_____

_____

Script Four

Describe: Hank, the company furnishes us with computers and software to assist us in doing our work.

Express: It's truly irresponsible of you to use your computer for writing the great American novel during working hours.

Specify: I want you to save your creative writing for your personal computer at home.

Question: What would happen if everyone here used their office computer for personal rather than work-oriented tasks?

_____

_____

_____

_____

_____

Script Five

Describe: Mr. Swanson, we have been your tenants here for almost eight years. During that time, we have asked only that you paint the apartment, and that was last year.

Express: I am aggravated that you have not only ignored our painting request but have just increased our rent by twenty percent.

Specify: I assume that you would like us to remain here. So, therefore, please forget the rent increase and paint the apartment as soon as possible.

Question: How would you like us to start looking for another place to live?

_____

_____

_____

_____

_____

Script Six

Describe: Andy, you really piss me off when you borrow my stuff and then forget to return it.

Express: I just spent twenty aggravating minutes looking for my circular saw, and guess who had it—you!

Specify: Leave my stuff alone.

Question: Next time, borrow from some other poor slob. Can you do that?

_____

_____

_____

_____

_____

Answers and Explanations to Chapter Seven Exercises

Script One Revised

Describe: Rosemary, there are many times when I ask for your assistance, and, although you are not busy, you refuse to help me.

Express: This makes me feel angry, because you are a part of this family and are responsible for participating in both the work and the fun activities.

Specify: I would like two hours of your time today to help me clean out the attic.

Question: What two hours can you give me?

Script One Analysis

In the describe line, the use of the phrase "you get huffy and nasty" will probably make Rosemary so angry that she will not even listen to the rest of the script. Always be as neutral as possible when describing the situation.

The express line is a good illustration of hiding behind an amorphous third party. It isn't the *family's* workload that is suffering from Rosemary's lack of cooperation, it is *your* workload. Moreover, when you hide behind amorphous third parties, you deny yourself one of the strongest tools you've got for getting Rosemary to cooperate, which is your personal relationship with her.

The specify line is not specific enough; it doesn't state what you want—which is Rosemary's help. Asking a person to *realize* or *understand* is not definitive. It leaves too much up in the air.

The question line does not provide closure. Moreover, it is insulting and critical. You want to say something that will invite dialogue or open the door to a change in behavior.

Script Two Revised

Describe: Jerry, often you take longer lunch breaks than the company rules allow.

Express: This makes me feel frustrated and angry, because it forces me to cut short my lunch time in order to cover your desk.

Specify: I want you to limit your lunch breaks to the allotted time frame of forty-five minutes.

Question: How do you suggest we solve this problem?

Script Two Analysis

The describe line is supposed to present a neutral picture of the problem. Telling Jerry he's inconsiderate is not neutral and will certainly not help the problem-solving effort.

Utilizing amorphous third parties weakens your argument. How do you know how everyone else feels? Besides, Jerry's long lunches are not affecting everyone—just you.

The specify line tells Jerry to get a watch, when you really want him to maintain a forty-five minute lunch schedule. Do you really care where or how he spends his lunch break?

This is not a question that invites discussion. It is a direct question that only requires a simple yes or no answer. Moreover, it does not indicate that a change in behavior is necessary.

Script Three Revised

Describe:	Alicia, although I've asked you to refrain from humming when we are working together, it still continues.
Express:	It makes me feel frustrated that I am unable to concentrate through your humming
Specify:	I want your help in solving this problem.
Question:	What ideas do you have that might allow you to hum and me to concentrate?

Script Three Analysis

Exaggerating the situation is not a good idea if your goal is to solve the problem. Just state the situation as it is. It's important here to figure who owns the problem. Don't blame Alicia because you require total silence in order to concentrate. Inflating the situation will not contribute to problem-solving. Alicia isn't doing a sing-along. She's only humming softly to herself. Moreover, she may not even be aware that she's even doing it. Give her the benefit of the doubt by asking her to help you solve *your* problem.

The question used can be answered with a simple yes or no" Therefore, it does not invite any discussion.

Script Four Revised

Describe:	Hank, frequently, after you have completed your work, I see you using your computer for a personal creative-writing project.
Express:	It makes me feel angry to see you using working hours in that manner.
Specify:	When you have free time, I want you to offer to assist others with their work.
Question:	How do you think your creative writing during working hours affects your image as a responsible professional worthy of promotion?

Script Four Analysis

Do not use the describe line to lecture Hank. Just state clearly what the problem is. The express line is for telling Hank how you feel when you see him engaged in his novel-writing during working hours. The specify line here is fine, except that it makes more sense to suggest how Hank might make better use of his free time.

Scrip Five Revised

Describe: Mr. Swanson, after living here for eight years, we asked you to paint the apartment, and that was last year. To date, you have failed to act on our painting request.

Express: I am aggravated because you have just increased our rent by twenty percent.

Specify: I want you to paint the apartment before your rent increase goes into effect.

Question: How soon can we expect our apartment to be painted?

Script Five Analysis

The describe line is adequate. However, the tying together of the notice of rental increase with the request for a paint job is more closely aligned in the revision. In the express line, the assumption is that Swanson has ignored your request. That may not be true. Repairs, especially painting, are done generally in the spring so the fumes can be let out through open windows.

The specify line is not the place to make assumptions and non explicit requests. Here you want to state what you want in terms as clear as possible. What weakens this script is that two requests are made in this line. It is always best if you focus on one item only—the most important one.

The last line is not a question, it is a threat. It would be unwise to make such a threat, unless you are 100 percent ready to follow through on it immediately. Swanson might get so angry upon hearing your threat that he might just ask you to get out immediately.

Script Six Revised

Describe:	Yesterday you borrowed my circular saw without telling me.
Express:	That made me extremely angry, because I needed it today and could not locate it.
Specify:	I do not want you to borrow anything of mine without asking me first.
Question:	How else will I know where my things have gone?

Script Six Analysis:

The describe line is so emotionally charged that Andy will never hear the rest of what is said. The express line does not really describe any personal feelings, although one can probably assume a good deal of anger from the tone of voice used in the delivery and the word *aggravating* in this line. The specify line is straightforward and clear. However, this being a neighbor, you might not want to suggest that no more borrowing will be allowed. You always want to appear reasonable. If he asks again, you can refuse his request to borrow.

Obviously, the question does not invite problem-solving or an understanding of the problem that Andy has created.

Chapter Eight

Your Body Language is Showing

RESEARCH STUDIES INDICATE THAT ONLY 7 percent of the message is delivered through words, while 93 percent is conveyed through body language and tone of voice. Such studies show that *understanding* happens:

- 7 percent from the meaning of the words
- 38 percent from the tone of voice
- 55 percent from the body language

How Others Understand What We Say

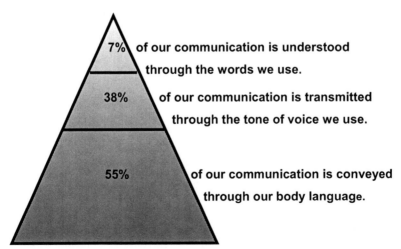

7% of our communication is understood through the words we use.

38% of our communication is transmitted through the tone of voice we use.

55% of our communication is conveyed through our body language.

If this is true, then communication is actually the act of the listener (person watching the speaker), *not* the speaker. It also reinforces the importance of monitoring your own body language, as well as watching your adversary's body language throughout your entire script. It is often said that true feelings are revealed through body language, while the words contain some manufactured acceptable pabulum that is only slightly related to the truth. Take this common exchange:

Husband: Are you angry with me?
Wife: No, I'm hurt.

Her body language gave her away. He knows she is angry, but she prefers to be manipulatively dishonest and make him feel guilty for something she refuses to identify.

When scripting to an adversary, you must make certain that your body language reflects your intent. Moreover, you want to project strength by taking the confrontation to your opponent. At work, early morning, before the day gets started, is the best time. Picture your adversary seated at his or her desk, drinking coffee. You walk into his or her office and, standing, deliver your script. Consider the relationship of height and power; you are standing, they are sitting—you are taking the power stance. If you approach your adversary later in the day, plan the seating arrangements in advance. Sitting opposite your adversary only reinforces the conflict, while sitting side by side delivers the message: "We are working on this conflict together."

When scripting in a close relationship, select a time when your adversary is relaxed and not under stress from a day at work or a difficult commute home or a miserable day with the children. Late in the evening is probably the best time. Always sit side by side.

Think of yourself as a tall oak tree with roots deep in the ground, unmovable. Your hands should be at your sides, relaxed, with palms opened (no clenched fists). Your face should reflect a serious demeanor.

Your voice should be strong and at an even pitch. You do not want to project any stress. This is why it is always a good idea to role-play with a friend before you confront the adversary. Practice does wonders for the nervous, pitch-varying speaker. Finally, always give your adversary 100 percent of your attention, along with a straight-in-the-eyeball look.

Estimating Your Stress Level

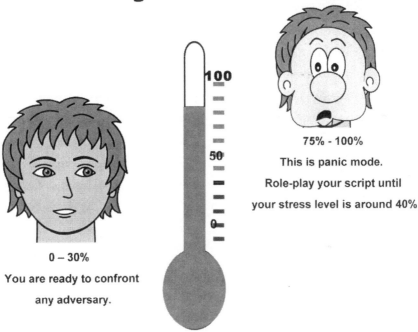

75% - 100%
This is panic mode.
Role-play your script until
your stress level is around 40%

0 – 30%
You are ready to confront
any adversary.

Now, let's consider the body language of the adversary. There are two significant items to notice in your adversary's body language, both of which are controlled by the adversary:

- changes in the physical distance between you
- the amount of continuous eye contact the adversary maintains with you

People lean toward what they like and away from what they don't like. This movement occurs at the moment the other person hears your words. The adversary may, after hearing your script, lean back in her chair, or push back against the chair, increasing the physical distance between you. Should the adversary come forward in her chair, you should anticipate hearing something positive. Should the adversary move away, you should assume you will quickly hear something negative with regard to your request.

The second cue involves your opponent's eye movements. The adversary should be giving you fairly uninterrupted direct eye contact all through the conversation. At some point in the interaction, the adversary may avert her eyes. She may suddenly become very absorbed in looking out the window or examining her hands or watching herself pick lint off her clothing. This is evidence that your adversary would like to get away from your speech. The physical constraints of the situation do not allow her to do that. So she escapes as much as she can by increasing the distance between you and herself or by directing her eyes and attention somewhere else.

In this confrontational format of communication, there is one moment of significant body language communication—immediately after you speak. At that moment, you will see before you the adversary's psychological response to your script reflected in a group of body language changes. Then your opponent will speak her response.

What you want to look for, immediately after you speak, is gross changes in the body language, followed quickly by a verbal response. If you see positive body language, anticipate hearing a positive response. If you see negative body language, anticipate hearing a negative response. The problem comes when you see negative body language but the response is positive. Then you know your opponent is not speaking truthfully. The adversary's body language and the words of the message that he or she speaks should match. If they do not, your adversary is not being honest.

VERBAL and NON-VERBAL COMPONENTS of BEHAVIOR

The messages we send with our body language	Non-Assertive "you can take advantage of me"	Assertive "I intend to stand my ground"	Aggressive "I am going to bully you"
Verbal	apologetic words hedging; failure to come to the point; rambling; veiled meanings; at a loss for words; not saying what you really mean.	clear statement of wants and feelings; objective words; saying what you mean; "I" messages.	"loaded" words; accusations; insinuations, subjective terms; "You" messages that blame or label; superior "know-it-all" declarations.
Non-Verbal	Body language instead of words; Others should guess what is meant; looking as if you don't mean what you say	attentive; self-assured; communicates caring, strength and firmness	exaggerated show of strength; flippant; sarcastic; air of superiority
Voice	weak, hesitant, soft, sometimes wavering.	firm, warm, well-modulated, relaxed, strong	tense, shrill, loud, cold, deadly quiet; demanding, superior.
Eyes	averted, downcast, teary, pleading	open, frank, level, direct eye contact.	expressionless, narrowed; cold, staring, unseeing.
Stance & Posture	lean for support; stooped; excessive head nodding.	well-balanced; straight forward; erect; relaxed	hands on hips; feet apart. still and rigid; rude
Hands	Fidgety, flutter, clammy.	relaxed motions, hands at side; palms open.	clenched; abrupt gestures; finger-pointing; fist pounding.

The most effective strategy for dealing with an adversary's body language is to comment on it directly, indicating that you *got* their unspoken message. Here are a few examples.

Adversary: *(Pushes back from the desk, leans back against the chair, crosses arms over chest, looks away into a far corner of the room, shrugs shoulders, looks back at you, rubs at her nose, and then says:)* I'll be happy to look into it and get back to you when I have some information.

You: I sense there is a big problem with my request and that your search for more information may be a delaying tactic, and I want …

Adversary: *(She pushes back in the chair, crosses her legs, averts eyes to the side wall, while she fidgets with a pen. When she looks back at you, her jaws seem tight. She responds in a strained voice:)* Well, I guess that might be possible.

You: You don't sound as if you want to make the effort to make it possible, and I want …

Adversary: *(She leans forward in the chair, smiles while giving you a straight-in-the-eyeball look, and says:)* I've been waiting for you to tell me you wanted more responsibility.

You: Well, I'm ready for a new challenge right now, and I want …

Spouse: *(Moves away from you, starts to pace the room while combing hair with fingers, and says:)* I don't want to discuss this right now.

You: I can see that this topic is stressful for you. Nevertheless, it's critical that we resolve this issue quickly. When would you like to discuss it, because I want …

Teenager:	*(Looks down at feet, hands clenching and unclenching, voice weak, and says:)* I'll try to not do that again.
You:	That doesn't sound like much of a commitment, and I want you to …

Body Language & Truthfulness

You speak your script.

> Your adversary's immediate reaction to your words is reflected by gross changes in his/her body language.

Your adversary responds verbally.

> Your adversary's body language and verbal response should match; if not, he/she is not speaking truthfully.

You respond to the body language message before you repeat the *specify line.*

some of the most commonly seen negative body language cues and what they mean.

Negative Body Language Cues	What that Body Language says
Fidgeting	discomfort
Teeth grinding	stress
Nervous laugh or cough	agitation
Reddening face	discomfort, embarrassment
Fluttering hand motions with long silences	discomfort; also reaction to making up a "story"
Hands at mouth	a desire to retract words just spoken
Arms crossed over chest	closed to discussion; negative reaction to your words
Rapid blink rate	untruthfulness
Hand touching nose	untruthfulness
Rubbing back of neck	aggravation; this is a pain in the neck
Combing hair with fingers	agitation
Pacing the floor	distancing him/herself from the issue
Playing with pen, paperclips, etc.	agitation; unwillingness to face the issue
Tapping pen or pencil in even cadence	impatience
Crossed legs, top one swinging	impatience
Hands clenching and unclenching	anger
Hands at throat	unexpected surprise
Hand rubbing chin	thinking; considering, evaluating

Negative Body Language Cues	What that Body Language says
Feet up on desk	prove it to me; I'm in charge here
Legs crossed one leg over the other	defensiveness
Bulging eyes	extreme anger
Purple-red face	extreme anger
Lack of eye contact	distancing him/herself from the issue
Rolling eyes to ceiling	heard this already; "Oh God, not this again"
Mumbling response	unsure, uncommitted
Voice high pitch, words rapid	panic, nervous
Voice low, words slow, deliberate	anger
Varying voice pitch	constructing a less-than-truthful response
Long silences	making up a response; deleting information
Sigh, noisy exhalation, groan	Passive-aggressive negative response; words will speak false agreement

Here is an example of how one partner, the wife, moves the conversation forward to getting what she wants and away from arguing by commenting on her husband's body language. Emily is the mother of four young children, who also works full time as a legal assistant. Cole is the owner of a small construction firm which has lately fallen on tough times. Both of them are concerned with conserving their financial resources. Emily wants to hire a housekeeper to come in once each week to help her with the housework. It is almost impossible for her to maintain a clean home environment while also working an eight-hour day. It is Saturday morning. Husband and wife are just finishing breakfast.

Emily:	For the past few months, I have told you that we need to hire a housekeeper. It makes me feel angry that you refuse to recognize I am simply too exhausted in the evenings to clean house. I want us to hire a housekeeper to come in one day each week. If you agree, it will relieve a lot of my stress.
Cole:	(*Pushes away from the table, rolls his eyes at the ceiling, and crosses his arms across his chest.*) I thought we were working on cutting expenses.
Emily:	I understand you believe you've heard this all before, but perhaps you haven't realized how exhausting it is for me to work a full eight-hour day and then attempt to clean house. I just cannot do it, and that's why I want us to hire a housekeeper to come in one day each week.
Cole:	(*Looks straight at her, arms still crossed over his chest.*) How much is this going to cost us?
Emily:	One hundred dollars each week.
Cole:	(*Stands up and begins to pace the floor.*) One hundred dollars—do you realize that's four hundred dollars a month?
Emily:	My sense is you regard that as a huge amount of money for housework. Actually, it is quite reasonable when you consider my health, and that's why I want us to hire a housekeeper to come in one day each week.
Cole:	(*Sits down, runs his fingers through his hair, and then makes fluttering gestures with his hands while looking off into space.*) Let's talk to the children; maybe they can help by doing more of the cleaning chores.
Emily:	I can plainly see that you already know that is not going to work long-term. I want us to hire a housekeeper to come in one day each week.

Cole:	*(Sighs, groans with head and eyes down, mumbles.)* All right, do what you want.
Emily:	Sweetie, this has to be *our* decision because it's *our* money. I need a strong commitment from you that you agree with this decision to hire a housekeeper for one day each week.
Cole:	*(Looks straight at her with fists clenched.)* I still think this is an unnecessary expense.
Emily:	I am aware that you are angry about this, but I simply cannot handle the house and a full-time job without some assistance. That's why I want us to hire a housekeeper to come in one day each week.
Cole:	*(Hands relax, and he looks straight at her.)* I understand and I agree. Your health is important, and so is a clean house. It's just a lot of money at a time when things are financially tight.
Emily:	Thanks for understanding. I'll hire someone today who will start next week.

Being appropriately
assertive gives you the
best chance of getting
what you want.

Chapter Eight Exercises

Directions: Assume you have just completed your script. Before your opponent responds verbally, he demonstrates the following combination of body language cues. In the space provided, interpret what the adversary is telling you with his body language cues.

1. The adversary leans back in his chair, smiles without looking at you, and puts his feet on the desk.

    _____

    _____

    _____

2. Your opponent gives a long sigh and then lowers his eyes to examine something on the desk or in his lap.

    _____

    _____

    _____

3. Your adversary's face becomes purple-red, his eye contact is 100 percent directed at you, and his eyes are wide open and bulging out.

    _____

    _____

    _____

4. Your opponent looks down at what he was doing before you spoke and continues with whatever he was doing.

    _____

    _____

    _____

5. Your adversary starts to pace back and forth across the room. His eyes are on the floor; he is rubbing the back of his neck.

    _____

    _____

    _____

6. Your opponent leans toward you, smiling; he is giving you direct, full eye contact.

    _____

    _____

    _____

Answers to Chapter Eight Exercises

1. The adversary's message is: "Prove it to me." However, he fully intends to say no to your request, no matter how much proof you bring to the table.

2. Whatever you asked of the opponent, he is unwilling to do it. However, he will tell you—insincerely—that he will try his best to do as you requested. Don't believe him.

3. Your opponent is extremely angry at what you said. To avoid some explosive hostility, it might be a good idea for you to put off further conversation and return with your same request another day. Give your opponent time to cool off. Since he has already heard your script once, he will listen next time.

4. This is extremely rude, pretending you are not even there. Your adversary wants you to go away so he doesn't have to deal with the issue you are presenting. Stand your ground and repeat your script.

5. Your adversary needs some perspective on the issue you are presenting. The issue is a difficult one for him. He may need a little time to figure things out. If you are patient and persistent, you will get what you want.

6. Your adversary is positive and willing to give you what you requested.

Chapter Nine

Sample Assertive Scripts

Full Conversational Scripts

The following pages contain a variety of scripts for both work and home situations. They are developed conversationally, so that you can hear how the scripting strategy might work in actual situations with a stubborn adversary. Always notice the manipulative tactics used by the adversary, as well as how the asserting person keeps returning to the crux of the matter until the adversary truly hears and understands the message.

Mgr:	Lou, today is the third time this month that I have given you an assignment that you either didn't do or turned in to me incomplete and poorly executed. This makes me feel angry and frustrated, because the quality of your work reflects on me as your supervisor, and you are making me look bad in the eyes of my manager. I want you to take back this report, redo it, and have it ready for me to review by 2:00 PM today. What reason do you have for consistently turning in poor quality work?
Lou:	Your instructions are never clear.
Mgr:	If you find that my instructions are not clear, you should come to me immediately and ask questions. So, tell me

	what's unclear about this assignment, because I want you to take back this report, redo it, and have it ready for me to review by 2:00 PM today.
Lou:	Everything's unclear.
Mgr:	Please be more specific, because I want you to take back this report, redo it, and have it ready for me to review by 2:00 PM today.
Lou:	All these reports you give me to do are so similar. Each one seems to just be a rehash of previous reports. I don't understand why there are so many of them.
Mgr:	Each report is designed for a different purpose and, often, a different audience, which I'm sure you already know. I want you to take back this report, redo it, and have it ready for me to review by 2:00 PM today.
Lou:	Can't you just give this one to somebody else to finish?
Mgr:	I don't think it's fair to expect others to correct your work. So, I want you to take back this report, redo it, and have it ready for me to review by 2:00 PM today.
Lou:	Do you ever assign these miserable reports to anyone else except me? Don't you think it would be nice to let others try their hand at these once in a while?
Mgr:	These reports comprise the major part of your job. Therefore, I want you to take back this report, redo it, and have it ready for me to review by 2:00 PM today.
Lou:	I hate doing them.
Mgr:	I get that. I understand that you really don't like doing these reports. Is this the message you've been trying to send me by doing the reports so poorly?
Lou:	*(mumbling)* Yes, I guess so.
Mgr:	Well, how are we going to solve this problem? These reports are your responsibility. I could agree to give you a greater variety of tasks, but how can I do that

when you are performing so badly on the tasks you've already got?

Lou: I see what you mean. I guess I should have told you outright how much I dislike doing these reports, but I was afraid that you would get angry and I might lose my job.

Mgr: Well, I am angry about your consistently poor quality work. But, more than that, we need to solve the immediate problem regarding this report, which I want you to take back, redo, and have ready for me to review by 2:00 PM today.

Lou: Okay, I'll rework it. Can we discuss putting more variety into my work at 2:00 PM today when I turn it in?

Mgr: I'd rather do that early in the morning, after I've reviewed your work on this report and after I've had time to consider what tasks I might assign to you that would be appropriate. Why don't we meet again next Tuesday morning at 10:00 AM? Meanwhile, I expect to see only quality work from you.

Lou: Okay! Thank you!

May: Fran, often you stop by my office to chat when I am scrambling to meet a deadline. This makes me feel uncomfortable, because it forces me to be impolite and ask you to go away. I want you to call and ask if I have the time to visit before you drop by. How else can I be both an effective employee and a good friend to you, by giving you my full attention when you do visit?

Fran: But I thought we were pals.

May: We are pals. But I want you to call and ask if I have the time to visit before you drop by.

Fran: But I really need talk to you *now*. You know that I'm going through some really difficult personal problems.

May:	Yes, I do know that, Fran. But I still want you to call first and ask if I have the time to visit before you drop by.
Fran:	Are you saying that you don't want to talk to me anymore?
May:	No, I do want to talk to you. It's just that when I'm busy, I cannot give you my full attention. That's why I want you to call first and ask if I have the time to chat before you stop by.
Fran:	So now I have to make an appointment. Some friend you turned out to be.
May:	Fran, you're making this very difficult. All I want is for you to call and ask if I have the time to visit before you stop by.
Fran:	*(whining)* All I want is a few minutes of your time. Is that so much to ask?
May:	I'm happy to give you a few minutes—even more, if you need it. It's just that I want you to call first and ask if I have the time to visit before you stop by.
Fran:	Is this how you repay me for all the times I put my work aside to hear your problems?
May:	But I always asked you first if you were busy, and that's really all I'm asking of you. I just want you to call first and ask if I have the time to visit before you stop by.
Fran:	So if I call and you're not busy, you'll talk to me.
May:	Yes, of course!
Fran:	So all you want me to do is call first.
May:	Yes!
Fran:	Okay. I'll call before I stop by.
May:	Thank you.
Buyer:	Two weeks ago I purchased this pressure washer from your store. Yesterday, the second time I used it, it jammed

and then started throwing sparks. This made me feel angry, because I had purchased what your salesperson told me was the best, top-of-the-line, and—of course—the most expensive, model. I want you to give me my money back. What else do you need to process a refund, other than my receipt?

Clerk: Are you sure you bought this in our store?

Buyer: Yes! Look at the receipt! I want you to give me my money back.

Clerk: Well, none of our other customers ever complained about this product.

Buyer: That may be, but I'm complaining about it, and I want you to give me my money back.

Clerk: Are you sure you put it together correctly? Perhaps you didn't follow the directions in its use. What were you doing with it, anyway?

Buyer: I was using it to clean off my patio. What difference does it make how I was using it? The unit is still under warrantee, and I want you to give me my money back.

Clerk: I know that. The warrantee information is right here on the box.

Buyer: So, what's the problem? For God's sake, will you just please give me my money back?

Clerk: Don't get testy with me, Lady. I'm sure the damage to the unit did not happen in this store. It must have been the way you were using it.

Buyer: I really don't want to argue with you about this. All I want is my money back. If you are not authorized to do that, then let me speak to your manager.

Clerk: I can offer you a replacement, in fact the same model you originally purchased. I'm sure we have another one in stock.

Buyer:	Why would I want another one when the first one malfunctioned? I want you to give me my money back.
Clerk:	We have a very good repair service. I can probably get them to work on your unit right away and you could pick it up day after tomorrow.
Buyer:	I don't want it repaired. I don't want it replaced. I want you to give me my money back.
Clerk:	Well, if you're sure I can't help you, then take the unit, your receipt, and this form to the second floor, where you'll find the Customer Service Department. They will refund your money.
Buyer:	Why didn't you tell me this in the first place? You could have saved us both a lot of time.
Dan:	Boss, I am already three months beyond the time for my performance appraisal. This really upsets me, because, until that paperwork is complete, I cannot get my annual increase. I would appreciate it if you could give me my performance appraisal by noon on Wednesday. What information will you need from me to complete the documentation by that time?
Boss:	I'm glad you stopped by. I wanted to speak to you about that marketing report we received from the St. Louis office.
Dan:	Certainly, we can do that, but first I'd like you to make plans for giving me my performance appraisal by noon on Wednesday.
Boss:	There are so many other things of greater priority right now. Surely you don't mind waiting another few weeks.
Dan:	Unfortunately, I do mind waiting. We are already three months late. So I would appreciate it if you could give me my performance appraisal by noon on Wednesday.

Boss:	I know I'm a little behind on that stuff, but you must realize how very busy I am right now.
Dan:	I certainly do recognize how busy you are. However, I would appreciate it if you could give me my performance appraisal by noon on Wednesday.
Boss:	Other people are waiting for their performance discussion, and none of them has made a fuss about the delay. Don't you think you're being a little unreasonable?
Dan:	I'm really not interested in what others are doing. I just want my performance appraisal by noon on Wednesday.
Boss:	I can't give you your appraisal until you give me some documentation on what you've accomplished this past year. You know that.
Dan:	I have that documentation right here. So, how about giving me my performance appraisal by noon on Wednesday
Boss:	*(sigh)* Okay. How does 2:00 PM on Wednesday sound?
Dan:	It sounds great. Thank you very, very much. See you then.
Ann:	Lee, yesterday you asked me if I would mind looking after your dog while you vacation in the Bahamas for a month. Your request makes me feel uncomfortable, because I dislike refusing you, but Sumo requires a lot of attention, and I already have a full-time job as well as my family to look after. I would appreciate it if you would ask someone else to take care of your dog. What other arrangements can you make for Sumo?
Lee:	I can't believe that you're actually saying no. It's not a big deal. All you have to do is walk through the hedge and put down one can of wet food, fill up his bowl of dry food, and make sure he has a fresh bowl of water.

It will take you all of five minutes. You can even leave him outside the entire time.

Ann: Lee, I do *not* want to look after your dog, so I would appreciate it if you would ask someone else to take care of Sumo.

Lee: You know how much he means to me; I can't leave his care to just anyone. It has to be someone who really likes dogs and who is dependable and trustworthy.

Ann: Thank you for the compliment. Nevertheless, I would appreciate it if you would ask someone else to take care of Sumo.

Lee: You know he really likes you. I think of all our friends and neighbors, you're his favorite.

Ann: That's nice, but I still would appreciate it if you would ask someone else to take care of Sumo.

Lee: Are you suggesting that I leave Sumo with strangers?

Ann: No. What I am suggesting is that you ask someone other than me to take care of Sumo.

Lee: I don't understand this. You've taken care of him so many times before. Why can't you do it now? Is it because I've waited until the last minute to ask? Or are you still angry that Sumo chewed up your sofa cushions the last time he was in your house?

Ann: The point is, I do not want to look after your dog this time. Please, ask someone else to take care of Sumo.

Lee: I tried to make arrangements for Sumo at the Doggie Marriott Kennel, but the cost would have bankrupted me. Can't you just do it for me this one time? Please?

Ann: Lee, you're not hearing me. I do not want to look after your dog this time. I want you to ask someone else to take care of Sumo.

Lee: Don't I always go out of my way to help you when you ask? Remember last winter when your car wouldn't start? Who drove you to and from work for three days? Me! And now, when I'm less than twenty-four hours from leaving, you refuse to look after my dog. Do you think that's how a good friend should act?

Ann: You have been there for me whenever I needed help, and I have been very appreciative and thankful for your friendship. However, looking after Sumo for thirty days is a huge responsibility. That's why I do not want to take care of your dog this time. I want you to ask someone else to take care of Sumo.

Lee: So it's the thirty days you object to?

Ann: Yes, thirty days is a very long time, and that's why I want you to ask someone else to take care of Sumo.

Lee: So if I were going away for a shorter period of time, you would take care of Sumo for me?

Ann: If it were for just three or four days, I'd be happy to look after Sumo. More than that would create difficulties for me. Therefore, this time I want you to ask someone else to take care of Sumo.

Lee: If I put Sumo in the kennel, would you at least go and visit him a few times while I'm away?

Ann: Yes, I can do that.

Lee: I know Sumo will appreciate that. Thanks.

Gil: Jack, I've asked you many times not to rummage through the papers on my desk, but you continue to do so, especially when I am out of the area. This makes me feel angry, because the information on those documents is often confidential and I am responsible for seeing that it remains that way. I want you never to go rummaging through the papers on my desk. How are we going to solve this problem?

Jack: Stop complaining! It's not a big deal. I just needed some information, and you weren't here, so I went looking for it.

Gil: If I'm not at my desk and you need something, you can leave me a memo, or you can wait until I return. I want you never to go rummaging through the papers on my desk.

Jack: Well, if the papers on your desk are so confidential, you should put them under lock and key instead of leaving them all over the place where anyone can see them.

Gil: You may have a point there. Nevertheless, I want you never to go rummaging through the papers on my desk.

Jack: It never occurred to me that you might be compulsive. I'm not going to steal any trade secrets, so what's your problem?

Gil: Apparently my problem is you. I want you never to go rummaging through the papers on my desk.

Jack: I think you're being unreasonable. Give you analysts a little authority and you're ready to take over the world.

Gil: That's not the issue. The issue is I want you never to go rummaging through the papers on my desk.

Jack: I'm not the only one around here that has problems dealing with you. The entire staff thinks you are inflexible and uncooperative.

Gil: We are not discussing how the staff feels about me. We are discussing the fact that you have no business reading the documents on my desk. I want you never to go rummaging through the papers on my desk.

Jack: This is not the CIA, you know.

Gil:	I do know that. Jack, I want you never to go rummaging through the papers on my desk.
Jack:	You're really serious about this, aren't you?
Gil:	Yes, I am, and I want you to never go rummaging through the papers on my desk.
Jack:	Okay. Okay.
Gil:	Thank you.
Jack:	I still think you ought to put them under lock and key.
Gil:	Thank you.

Boss:	Sue, at least three days each week you come to work late. That makes me feel angry, because I have to answer your phones until you get here, and I don't get paid to do your job. I want you in here every day by 8:30 AM. What will you do to solve this problem?
Sue:	I'm not the only one around here who comes in late. Phil gets in here after I do, and I don't see you talking to him.
Boss:	Sue, we are not talking about Phil. We are talking about you, and I want you in here every day by 8:30 AM.
Sue:	You know I always stay late to make up the time. Why, yesterday I was here until after 6:00 PM.
Boss:	We are not talking about when you leave. We are talking about when you arrive, and I want you in here every day by 8:30 AM.
Sue:	The traffic is really horrendous coming in from the north. You know that! And I have no control over the traffic.
Boss:	I know you don't have any control over the traffic. I also know that it is especially bad coming in from the north. Nevertheless, I want you in here every day by 8:30 AM.

Sue:	It's not like I'm doing this on purpose. I have kids that need to be dropped off at school and day care before I come on in.
Boss:	I do understand that your mornings are complicated. However, I want you in here every day by 8:30 AM.
Sue:	I don't see the problem. I may be a little late, but I do get all my work done. Are you unhappy with the quality and quantity of my work?
Boss:	I am very happy with your work. Your work is not the problem. Your arrival time is the problem, and I want you in here every day by 8:30 AM.
Sue:	I didn't think getting in here exactly by 8:30 AM. was such a big deal.
Boss:	Well it is, and I want you in here every day by 8:30 AM.
Sue:	(sigh) I guess I'll just have to get up a whole lot earlier in the morning.
Boss:	That sounds like a good plan. Do I have your commitment that you will be in here every day by 8:30 AM?
Sue:	Well … I'll certainly try.
Boss:	I want you to do more than try. I want you to actually be here every day by 8:30 AM.
Sue:	What do you want, a commitment in writing?
Boss:	No. What I would like is to hear you make a strong statement about your intentions, rather than a wishy-washy "I'll try."
Sue:	Okay! Okay! I'll be here.
Boss:	Thank you!

Sample Scripts without the Subsequent Dialogue

Describe:	Boss, last week you assigned Tommy Lee Bonze, who's a smoker, and me to work as a team on the advertising research report. I was delighted to step up to the challenge.

Express: Now, however, I feel used because I'm doing most of the work while Tommy Lee goes on break after cigarette break.

Specify: I want you to tell Tommy Lee to cut his cigarette breaks to four ten-minute breaks per day.

Question: What else can be done to encourage Tommy Lee to spend more time working and less time smoking?

Describe: Boss, I have asked you many times for more challenging assignments, but I continue to get the same old boring tasks.

Express: This makes me feel frustrated and anxious, because I am not growing professionally.

Specify: I want you to give me full responsibility for training the department in the use of the new LS400 software system and the archive project which will follow the LS400 rollout.

Question: What other responsibilities might you assign to me that would help me grow professionally?

Describe: Two months ago, when I told you about all the problems I was having with Tom Muse's performance, you asked me to make more of an effort at coaching him.

Express: It makes me feel frustrated that, in spite of all my efforts, Tom's performance and attitude have not improved. Moreover, his continued presence is demoralizing my staff.

Specify: I want your support and guidance in taking the necessary steps to terminate Tom's employment.

Question: What steps can we take to secure Tom's prompt termination?

Describe:	Bill, whenever we go out for lunch together, you order a much more expensive dish than I do and then insist that we split the bill.
Express:	This makes me feel used and angry, because I'm paying more than my fair share.
Specify:	I want you to treat me to lunch our next three times out together to even up the score.
Question:	How does that solution sound to you?
Describe:	Last week at a staff meeting, the boss assigned you the Gatewell project, saying it was to be completed by the next staff meeting, which is tomorrow. Today, I found that project on my desk with a yellow sticky on it saying PLEASE HANDLE.
Express:	This confuses me, because the boss has not told me to assist you.
Specify:	I want you to go through the boss if you need my assistance.
Question:	How else can I possibly squeeze in your work when I already have a full plate of priorities?
Describe:	George, this morning you asked me to corroborate your story to your wife that we will be working late every night this week on a special project.
Express:	This makes me feel uncomfortable. Besides, I am a lousy liar.
Specify:	I want you to ask someone else to help you with your story.
Question:	What kind of difficulties might I get you into if your wife figured out I was lying?

Describe: Donna, frequently you ask me about something, and, if you do not like my answer, you go to another staff member to see if he or she will give you a different response.

Express: This irritates me, because it appears as if you are trying to play one of us against another.

Specify: I would appreciate it if you would either accept the answers I give you or stop asking me questions altogether.

Question: Which will you do?

Describe: Harriet, often when you request data from my area, you put a big red RUSH on your request—even when it is not an emergency situation.

Express: This makes me feel stressed and angry, because I provide data to sixteen other areas of the organization, whose needs are every bit as critical as yours.

Specify: I want you to stop putting pressure on me to reorder my priorities in your favor by using the rush notation on every task.

Question: How can we make the rush issue work more effectively for both of us?

Describe: Carl, last week when my car wouldn't start, you generously offered me a ride home. However, on the way home, you made unwanted advances.

Express: That made me feel uncomfortable and frustrated, because I consider you a friend and certainly do not want to make a harassment complaint against you.

Specify: I want your simple promise that such overtures will never happen again.

Question: How does that solution sound to you?

Sample Scripts for Managers Addressing Performance Issues with Staff
The scripts in this next section illustrate how the script format can be used when managers and supervisors speak with individual staff members about performance issues. Please notice that each script states very clearly what exactly is wrong and how it might be corrected. The intention of each script is to be tough on the issues—but respectful of the person.

Describe: Trey, I've asked you six times in the last four months to have your weekly activity reports complete and on my desk by Wednesday at noon. However, the data always arrives late.

Express: This makes me feel angry, because, when your data is late, my reports to my manager are delayed, causing me embarrassment and needless explanations to those whose work depends upon that information.

Specify: I want you to give me your completed weekly project reports by Wednesday noon each week.

Question: How can I assist you in making certain that those reports are on time from now on?

Describe: Gerry, often when you have questions relating to your work, instead of trying to figure things out for yourself, you come to me.

Express: This makes me feel concerned and baffled, because you're smart and well trained.

Specify: If you decide to ask for my assistance, I want you to bring three suggestions with you for solving the problem.

Question: What other ideas do you have for strengthening your confidence and competence?

Describe: Matt, frequently when you are upset about something, you speak in a loud and angry voice. Even though you've been told this is not acceptable behavior, it continues.

Express: This makes me feel aggravated and angry, because it forces me to spend time cleaning up all the emotional debris that you leave in your wake.

Specify: I want you to express yourself in every situation as if you were speaking to the president of the company.

Question: What else can you do to do to foster an image as an emotionally responsible and mature professional?

Describe: Vivienne, last month during your performance discussion, you gave me your word that, in an effort to raise your productivity level, you would limit your personal phone calls and visiting of co-workers to lunch and coffee breaks.

Express: It annoys and infuriates me that you have made little effort to keep your promise and that your productivity continues to deteriorate.

Specify: I want you to give me a written plan of action within the next three days that states specifically how you will turn this situation around.

Question: How quickly can you have that action plan completed?

Describe: Four weeks ago, I promoted Denzil Wasserman, instead of you, to senior analyst. Since then, I've seen a dramatic and negative change in your demeanor and productivity level.

Express: This disturbs me greatly, because I thought your career aspirations involved leadership, not analytical work.

Specify: I want you to modify your conduct so that you behave like the leader you wish to be.

Question: How else can I consider you for a leadership position?

The dilemma for most managers is this. They know that they must be strong and direct in order to achieve results. They also realize that being strong may be perceived as aggressiveness. That perception would generate more problems than it would solve. Therefore, the tendency is to err in the other direction, by stating the issue so tactfully with suggestions and hints that the employee never really does understand what the problem is. In truth, most employees appreciate an honest and straightforward feedback session regarding their performance shortcomings, as long as they do not feel castigated or condemned in the process. The following story illustrates how, when a manager made an effort to be courteous, his message was totally lost on the employee.

George was the best salesperson the company had. In fact, he was phenomenal. However, George had a heavy, fast-growing beard. By 10:00 each morning, he looked as if he had not shaved in three days. Clients consistently complained about his slovenly appearance. Here is how the boss addressed the issue:

Boss:	George, what kind of shaving apparatus do you use?
George:	I like a straight razor, specifically, Gillette.
Boss:	Have you ever considered an electric or battery-operated portable razor? You know, one you could use in the car if you had to.
George:	Oh no. I like the old lather-up-over-the-sink routine. It kind of wakes me up in the morning.
Boss:	Well, if you carried a portable with you, you could always clean up a little if you had to. You know, before you saw each customer.
George:	That's true, but I'm an old-fashioned guy.
Boss:	Are you troubled about your heavy beard?
George:	That's exactly why I use a straight razor.

Sample Scripts for Confronting Issues at Home

The main difficulty about raising issues at home using the assertive script is that the personal risks are always higher than they are at work. These are often the people who mean the most to you in your life. Once again, the tendency is to hold things inside and hope that time will somehow make the situation better. There are only two things that happen with time:

- you become more aggravated
- the situation becomes worse.

Never do the problems just go away. You have to address the issues just as you would at work—with clarity, brevity and, above all, respect.

Describe:	Honey, as you well know, things are pretty tight financially right now.
Express:	It aggravates me that the credit card bills keep moving in the wrong direction.
Specify:	I want you to limit your spending to the essentials of food, gas, and such.
Question:	What other suggestions do you have that will help limit our expenditures?
Describe:	Ernesto, last month you brought home a boy who had been in trouble with the authorities for drug possession. Last week, it was a girl with questionable morals. Yesterday, it was someone who had been expelled from school for cheating.
Express:	Your recent choice of friends distresses me and causes me anxiety, because you seem unable to select friends who will support you in maintaining an honorable, ethical, trustworthy, and responsible life.
Specify:	I want you to make a written list of the qualities you think are important to have in a close friend, so that we can discuss your list together.

Question: How soon can you have that list completed?

Describe: Anna, every weekend you and I exchange angry words regarding the condition of your room. Each time you tell me that if I don't like looking at the mess to simply close the door.

Express: This makes me feel furious and frustrated, because your room is in my house, and the expensive clothes on your bedroom floor were purchased with my hard-earned dollars.

Specify: I want you to clean up your room today before lunch, and I want you to keep it clean from now on

Question: What difficulties do you anticipate making that happen?

Describe: Son, last week you returned my new car with several fresh dents and no explanation as to how they got there. Now you are asking to borrow the car again.

Express: It makes me feel angry that you have so little respect for my things.

Specify: I want you to stop asking me if you can borrow my car.

Question: What would you do if I borrowed something valuable of yours, damaged it, gave no explanation or apology, and then asked to borrow it again?

Describe: I have asked you many times to telephone me if you are going to be late for dinner, but you never do.

Express: This makes me feel angry, because it appears as if you have no respect for my time or cooking efforts.

Specify: I want you to tell me how we can solve this problem.

Question: What can we do?

Describe: Every time we start into a lovemaking session, you mention your ex.

Express: This makes me feel uncomfortable, and I get the impression that you'd rather be with him (or her).

Specify: I want you to stop mentioning other people when we make love.

Question: How would you feel if I started talking about former romantic escapades at a time like that?

Describe: Whenever I get ready to leave for the gym to go exercise, you find some reason to delay me.

Express: This makes me feel confused, because you acknowledge the importance of me exercising and losing weight, yet your actions say something very different.

Specify: I want you to support me in leaving the house for aerobic class by 7:30 every evening.

Question: How exactly will you do that?

Describe: Mom, Dad, whenever you come to visit us, you bring lots of candy for the children, even though we've asked you not to.

Express: This makes me feel aggravated and stressed, because the kids say I am a hateful parent when I take the candy away.

Specify: I want you to help me preserve the children's health and teeth by *not* giving them candy.

Question: What other kinds of things can you give the children that would be healthy?

Describe: Mr. Rogers, at least three times each week, your German shepherd, Tiny Tim, comes into my yard to do his business.

Express:	It makes me feel furious and enraged to see him tearing up my grass and killing my shrubs, which I try so hard to keep looking nice.
Specify:	I want you to keep Tiny Tim out of my yard.
Question:	What will you do to ensure that Tiny Tim stays out of my yard?

Describe:	Harry, last month you borrowed my saber saw, broke it, and replaced it with a much cheaper model. Last week you borrowed my ratchet wrench and returned it damaged. Now you want to borrow my extension ladder.
Express:	This makes me feel uncomfortable, because not only might you damage the ladder, you might also hurt yourself with it.
Specify:	I want you to stop asking me if you can borrow my tools.
Question:	How about going to Rent-A-Center to get the tools you need?

Describe:	Mr. Fairwrench, when I brought my car in for service, you gave me this written estimate of $378.00. Now that the work is done, you present me with a bill for $1,058.75.
Express:	It makes me feel used and angry that your bill is more than double the estimate. Moreover, you never contacted me to say the car needed additional work or that you had underestimated the cost of the service.
Specify:	I want you to revise your bill so that it more closely approximates your original estimate.
Question:	What exactly did you do to the car that made the service so costly?

Describe: Mike, Katie, every night we have an angry discussion about doing your homework before watching any TV.

Express: It makes me feel angry that, after a hard day at work, I have to face this unpleasantness with you every single night.

Specify: I want you to comply—without argument—with the principle to which we all agreed: all homework must be completed before any TV watching takes place.

Question: Since you both hope to go to college, how important is it for you to get good grades now?

Describe: Doctor, my child has a temperature of 103, you're giving him a "little something to make him feel better," which I assume is a narcotic, and you tell me not to worry.

Express: This makes me feel uncomfortable, because it seems as if you think I'm not intelligent enough to understand medical terminology.

Specify: I want you to tell me specifically what you are prescribing for my child and explain exactly what is wrong with him.

Question: What exactly is wrong with my son?

Describe: Rabbi Schwartz, I have just received a letter from you stating that, based on your estimate of my income, I should donate a specific amount to the building fund.

Express: This aggravates me, because, while I recognize your need for funds, I do not understand how you can presume to tell me how much to donate.

Specify: I would appreciate it if you would stop sending out such letters to me.

Question: I will give what I determine is suitable. How will that work for you?

Describe: Mom, whenever I bring Harrison Lincoln home with me, you hardly acknowledge his presence, even though you know he's been my "significant other" for the past two years.

Express: It makes me feel irritated and annoyed that you seem unable to accept that your thirty-year-old daughter has the right to make her own relationship decisions.

Specify: When I bring Harrison over for dinner next week, I want you to treat him as if he were a very good and close friend.

Question: What else will you do to show Harrison that you accept and respect him?

Describe: Olga, last Saturday you dropped off your three little toddlers at 10:00 AM, telling me you had a little shopping to do and would be back to retrieve them before 1:00 PM. However, you did not return until 6:00 PM.

Express: That made me feel used and furious, because I work all week and need my Saturdays to clean, shop, go to the cleaners, and so on. I did not expect to be babysitting and feeding your children for the day.

Specify: I want you to never again drop off your children for me to look after.

Question: What were you thinking when you told me it would only be three hours?

Describe: Uncle Robby, whenever you come to visit, you pick up little Clio, hug her, kiss her, and rub her front and her bottom.

Express: This makes me fell frustrated and angry, because my little girl does not enjoy being handled that way, and because I have asked you several times not to do that.

Specify:	I want you to refrain from picking up Clio and putting your hands on her.
Question:	In what other ways can you show her that you are happy to see her?

Describe:	Honey, six weeks ago I asked you to fix the garage door, but that still has not been done.
Express:	That makes me feel anxious and concerned, because it forces me to leave our new car parked out in the elements.
Specify:	I want you to fix the garage door this weekend.
Question:	Who will you ask to help you?

Chapter Nine Exercises

Directions: In the following problem situations, design a script so that each one follows the blueprint below.

1. State the problem clearly, utilizing specific data.
2. Avoid subjective terms or disparaging words.
3. Declare how you feel without denigrating yourself.
4. Refrain from hiding behind amorphous third parties.
5. Announce clearly what you want as an outcome of the discussion.
6. Address only one issue.
7. Finish with an open-ended question that encourages problem-solving.

The suggested scripts will be found following the exercise.

1. Your younger brother has defaulted on a loan for which you co-signed, and the bank is threatening to put a garnishment on your wages unless you bring the payments up to date. You are being seriously considered for a promotion; a garnishment would probably kill your chances for promotion. You are a single parent with two children to support. You need the raise.

_____

_____

_____

_____

_____

2.   Several weeks ago, while you were out visiting a new client, one of your co-workers handled an emergency telephone call from your best client. Your helpful co-worker calmed the client down and resolved his problem. Today this client called in and asked for your co-worker. This client represents big dollars to you, and you do not want to lose him. Your co-worker is, of course, delighted to step in and take over. You suspect she is trying to steal your client

_____

_____

_____

_____

_____

3.   You are one of two supervisors in the department. You are very strict with your staff regarding the rules, while the other supervisor is very lax. For example, many of her staff are rarely there by 8:30, and others are as much as thirty minutes late. You insist that all your people are there and ready to work by 8:30 sharp. Every Friday afternoon at 3:00, there is a supervisors' meeting. When you return at 4:20, your people are still working. The other supervisor's staff are gone by 3:45, except for one person who stays to answer the phones. The lax enforcement of the rules by the other manager makes you look unreasonable. Your people are complaining.

_____

_____

_____

_____

_____

4. You are the senior manager in your area. Today, Lily Byers, the team leader in one of the administrative groups, told you that her supervisor, Tim Dunne, has been giving most of his attention to one of the new clerks. She said, "It seems as if he has no time for any one else. I hate to say he's playing favorites, but that sweet young thing is getting all the plum assignments. The way he's treating the rest of us—it feels like discrimination."

_____

_____

_____

_____

_____

5. You took this job because it paid well and the tasks involved were similar to previous jobs. What you didn't realize, however, was the lack of management structure provided. Your manager gives you very little direction; he/she wants the staff to work on their own and solve their own problems. Last week, you were very embarrassed at a staff meeting. You were evidently expected to provide certain reports. Your boss had never told you those reports were required, what they should contain, or how they were to be laid out.

_____

_____

_____

_____

_____

6. You are in the fifth year of your second marriage. Your spouse has an older boy from a previous marriage, who is living with you. The boy is a high school dropout who is currently unemployed. You have just learned that his girlfriend is pregnant. You would like to avoid upsetting your spouse, but you want that boy out of your house before he decides to bring his girlfriend and their baby home for you to support.

_____

_____

_____

_____

_____

7. Your boss, "Silent Sam" Stafford refuses to speak to you; he communicates by e-mail. You get no feedback, so you are never sure if he is pleased with your work. When you asked for feedback, Sam's response was, "You're not stupid; you should know if what you're doing is all right without me telling you." When you asked for a meeting to discuss expanding your role in the department, Sam said he didn't have time.

_____

_____

_____

_____

_____

8. While cleaning up your daughter's room, you discover a stash of drugs. You are horrified. Your daughter is an honor student. She is also a member of the girls' basketball team. You are fairly certain you know most of her close friends. As a parent, you have tried to be vigilant without being intrusive. You wonder what could have happened.

_____

_____

_____

_____

_____

Suggested Responses to Chapter Nine Exercises

1. Your first step should be to explain things to your brother and see if you and he together can bring his payments to the bank current.

Describe: Bro, I have received a notice from the bank threatening to garnishee my wages, because payments on the car loan I co-signed for you are in arrears.

Express: This troubles and angers me, because a garnishment will cost me the promotion for which I am being considered.

Specify: I want the two of us to pool the necessary funds to bring that loan up to date today.

Question: How much money will you contribute?

2. Although you are probably correct in your suspicions that your co-worker is trying to steal your client, it is always a good idea to give the other person the benefit of the doubt.

Describe: Beth, I understand that my client Grabbit, Grabbit, and Runn called in today and asked for you instead of me.

Express: That makes me feel somewhat confused, because, although I am delighted that you were able to assist them in my absence, I am the contact of record.

Specify: I want you to give me all the details of their recent phone call, so that I can service their needs.

Question: What exactly was the nature of their call?

3. This is not a situation that can be resolved at your level. You need to speak with your boss. Get some clarity on how strictly your boss wants you to enforce the company's rules. Then you can request that the boss make that decision apply equally to all supervisors.

Describe: Boss, I have always insisted that my staff arrive and leave at the scheduled times each day. Because other supervisors have been less strict, my staff is now complaining that I am inflexible and rigid.

Express: This concerns and confuses me, because I'd like to enforce the rules without looking like a tyrannical boss.

Specify: I would appreciate it if you could please clarify how closely you expect me to enforce the rules.

Question: How strict should I be regarding arrival and departure times?

4. Discrimination complaints are messy; you want to avoid them if at all possible. Your first step is to make Tim Dunne aware of the situation his behavior may be creating.

Describe: Tim, I understand that Suzie Sweets, because she lacks experience, may be requiring more than her fair share of your time.

Express: This concerns me greatly, because it may appear to others as if you are playing favorites.

Specify: I want you to make sure that you spend as much time with your other staff members as you do with Suzie.

Question: How much time do you give Suzie as compared with your other staff members?

5. This situation could result in a poor performance evaluation. Therefore, you must speak to the boss immediately. Ask for more structure with regard to his/her expectations.

Describe: Boss, because I am new to this job, I need a little extra guidance in terms of your expectations for my performance.

Express: I feel distressed that I was not prepared at our last staff meeting and that I let you down.

Specify: I want you to tell me exactly what reports you require of me, what they should contain, and how you prefer them to be presented.

Question: How soon can we have that discussion?

6. Obviously your spouse lost his/her ability to influence the son a long time ago, so speaking with the spouse will only get him/her aggravated. Your best chance of making a change in the situation is to speak to the son.

Describe: Son, now that you are about to become a family man, it is time for you to find a well-paying job and a place for your little family to live.

Express: It concerns me that you have made the decision to start a family at such a young age. However, many others have done the same, so I will not worry about you.

Specify: I want you to leave this house within the next ninety days, so that you have sufficient time to get settled in your own place before the baby comes.

Question: Which will you concentrate on first: finding a job or locating a place to live?

7. With a boss like this, your career is at a standstill. Sam is not a "people-person" and has no interest in helping you grow. You should look for a new job. However, if you want to give Silent Sam one more chance to support your career growth, here is an appropriate script.

Describe: Sam, without specific feedback from you, I am unable to improve my performance or grow into greater responsibility.

Express: This makes me feel angry and frustrated, because, without your coaching, my career is dead in its tracks.

Specify: I want the two of us to have a serious face-to-face discussion regarding my present performance and future career growth.

Question: How quickly can we do that?

8. Before speaking to your daughter, you need to make certain your stress level is under control. This is a situation where you may want to role-play with a friend before you confront your daughter.

Describe: While cleaning up your room yesterday, I came across this (hold out the stash).

Express: I was both distressed and surprised to learn that you have decided to put your honor student designation and your sports success in jeopardy.

Specify I want you to explain your decision about doing drugs to me.

Question: How did you decide to start using drugs?

Chapter Ten

Escalating a Script

As you have seen in the previous section of sample scripts, after the initial script is spoken, you simply keep repeating that third line, *the specify line*, where you state what it is you want. This technique is called *the broken record*. It is utilized because your adversary may attempt to change the subject. At other times, your adversary may use criticism to divert you from the subject and onto defending yourself. Most often, however, your adversary is busy mentally trying to think up a response. Whatever the reason, the result is the same. Your adversary has so much going on in her head that she has not really heard what you are trying to tell her. Therefore, you have to repeat yourself several times.

Plan on repeating your specify line several times or until you get an appropriate response. This may take as many as four repetitions. An effective way to begin the escalation process is to start by saying "I'd *like* you to ...," and then switch to "I *want* you to ..." if, after two repetitions, you do not get a satisfactory response from your opponent. One note of caution here: as soon as your adversary gets your message, you should stop using the broken record. To continue using it after your message has been received would be considered extremely aggressive.

The second method for escalating a script involves the way you phrase the question at the end of your script. To illustrate, let's take the following script.

Describe: Bill, three days ago, in the parking lot, you damaged the right rear bumper of my new car.

Express: It makes me feel angry that so far you have neither acknowledged the damage nor offered to pay for the repairs.

Specify: I would appreciate it if we could discuss how you wish to handle this problem today.

Question: When can we get together?

Here is the same script escalated.

Describe: Bill, three days ago, in the parking lot, you damaged the right rear bumper of my new car.

Express: It makes me feel angry that so far you have neither acknowledged the damage nor offered to pay for the repairs.

Specify: I want to know today how you intend to handle this problem.

Question: What are *you* going to do about the damage to my car?

There are actually five levels of intensity you can use in the question.

1. Request a discussion without pressing for immediate closure.
   What would be a convenient time for us to talk about this?
   When would you like to get together to work this thing out?
2. Put yourself into the problem-solving process.
   How can I help you with this?
   What can we do to resolve this issue?

3. Leave it all up to the other person.

    What will you do to resolve the problem?

    How do you intend to handle this?

4. Press for your closure.

    What assurances can you give me that this will never occur again?

    What documentation do you need from me to make this happen?

5. Offer a false choice (*very* manipulative).

    Do you wish to resolve this now, or shall we resolve this at 2:00 PM today?

    Which would you like to do first: clean your room or do your homework?

Script Levels

So far, all the scripts you have learned about have ended in a question. This was done in order to invite the other person to participate in the conversation and negotiate a satisfactory solution for both parties. It is called a *Level I Script*. Of all the scripts, it is the most useful, and therefore recommended for most situations.

TIPS FOR DESIGNING ASSERTIVE SCRIPTS*

*Adapted from **Asserting Yourself** by Sharon and Gordon Bower, Addison-Wesley, 1986.

ALWAYS

Describe the other person's behavior objectively

Use concrete terms

Describe a specific time, place & frequency

Describe the person's actions, not the *motive*

Express your feelings

Verbalize your feelings calmly

Speak positively as if there is a goal to
be achieved

Address the specific offending behavior

Ask for a specific change in the person's behavior

Request only one or two changes at a time

Specify the actions you want stopped or performed

Consider if the person can comply without harming
themselves in some way

If appropriate, specify what changes you will make to
ensure an agreement

NEVER

Assume to know the other person's motives

Use abstract, vague terms

Generalize by using terms such as *always* or *never*

Guess at what the other person was thinking

Deny your feelings

Unleash an emotional outburst

State your feelings negatively, make put-down or attackin
and insulting remarks

Attack the character of the person

Merely imply that you'd like a change

Ask for too large a change

Ask for many changes simultaneously

Ask for changes using nebulous traits or qualities

Ignore the other person's needs by only seeking your ow
satisfaction

Think that only the other person has to alter their actions

Practitioners of assertive communication affirm that being properly assertive will ensure you get everything you want. Actually, being properly assertive gives you the *best chance* of getting what you want. However, there are no guarantees. Without the willing participation and cooperation of your adversary, getting even a portion of what you want is almost impossible.

Being appropriately assertive gives you the best chance of getting what you want.

However, there is no reason why you have to resolve a problem the first time you attempt a confrontation. There is always tomorrow, and the day after that, and so on. Suppose you attempted a script today and your adversary flatly refused to discuss the matter with you. Utilizing the idea of the broken record, you might return the following day and begin your script all over again. Should that fail to get some movement from your adversary, return yet again on the next day and begin your script all over again. Your adversary will quickly learn three things:

- You are *very* serious about the matter in question.
- You are an absolute pest and a consummate heckler.
- If they want you to go away, they will have to deal with you.

You may run across situations in which you do not want to negotiate—where it is critical that you get what you want if at all possible. Then, too, there may be circumstances when you fear the other person might react aggressively to your script. In those situations, you may want to consider the use of an alternate script—one that ends in positive consequences. This would be a *Level II Script*.

Here is the parking lot incident redone in a Level II Script format, including the positive consequences (Pos Con).

Describe:	Bill, three days ago, in the parking lot, you damaged the right rear bumper of my new car.
Express:	It makes me feel angry that so far you have neither acknowledged the damage nor offered to pay for the repairs.
Specify:	I *would like* us to discuss how you intend to handle this problem today.
Pos Con:	If we settle this quickly, the accident will not negatively affect our friendship.

Level II Scripts, which end in positive consequences, are very effective in the work situation, especially if the consequences you choose relate to human relations factors. Such scripts are not, however, successful in family situations. Perhaps it is because those closest to you feel entitled to take advantage of you now and then.

Ending a script with a negative consequence (this is called *a Level IV Script)* will be perceived as a (take-it-or-leave-it) threat. This will immediately polarize the position of your adversary, making negotiation impossible. It is ill advised in any situation to design a script that sounds like a threat (a Level IV Script). It is possible, however, to design a script that prompts the other person to speak the negative consequences. This allows you to say that you don't want that outcome to occur and to restate your preferred outcome. This is a *Level III Script.*

Here again is the same damaged-car script, but in a Level III format.

Describe: Bill, three days ago, in the parking lot, you damaged the right rear bumper of my new car.

Express: It makes me feel angry that so far you have neither acknowledged the damage nor offered to pay for the repairs.

Specify: *I want* us to discuss how you intend to handle this problem today.

Rethink: What do you think is likely to occur if you continue to avoid talking with me about this?

Bill Responds: What are you going to do, sue me?

Re-specify: Bill, that's the last thing I want to do. You're a good friend, and I'm sure this was simply an unfortunate accident. That's why I want us to discuss how you intend to handle this problem today.

Question: What do you want to do?

Ending a script with a negative consequence will be perceived as a take-it-or-leave-it threat.

This will quickly polarize your adversary making negotiation impossible.

Of course, if you choose, you can always end a script with negative consequences. This is the *Level IV Script*. This is the take-it-or-leave-it stance, and it will be heard by your adversary as a threat. Therefore, you stand a strong chance of doing more harm than good with its use. The best advice would be to *never* use negative consequences—unless you are prepared to lose both the possibility of solving the problem and your relationship with the other person. Here again is the same damaged car script in a Level IV format, including the negative consequences (Neg Con).

Describe: Bill, three days ago, in the parking lot, you damaged the right rear bumper of my new car.

Express:	It makes me feel angry that so far you have neither acknowledged the damage nor offered to pay for the repairs.
Specify:	*I want* us to discuss how you intend to handle this problem today.
Neg Con:	If you continue to avoid speaking with me about this, you leave me no choice but to sue you in court for the cost of the repairs.

Bill could respond, "Oh yeah? You just go right ahead and sue, and I'll counter sue. You have no proof that I'm the one who hit your car."

As you can see, there is a regular progression to escalating a script. The key to successful scripting, however, really depends upon remaining at Levels I, II, and III. Most important of all: if you are aggravated about something, do not wait too long to address the problem. The longer you wait, the more stress is generated, and the more likely it is that you will find yourself at Level IV.

Often, the stress buildup producing a Level IV reaction is seen between parents and teenagers. Just suppose for a moment that you catch your teenager smoking marihuana in the house. You explode, screaming, "If I ever catch you smoking that stuff again, I'm going to throw you out of the house!" Since your son is a red-blooded American boy, what do you think he is going to do? Right! Let you catch him smoking weed in the house again.

Now that he has called your bluff, will you actually throw the kid out into the street? If you do not follow through on your threat and actually throw him out, does it mean that it is now okay for your teenager to smoke weed in the house? Don't make Level IV threats unless you are fully prepared to follow through. Although speaking from Level IV may sound strong, it is actually a very weak position, because you have left yourself no negotiating room. There is no Level V position.

Think of the employee who, in a moment of rage about some aspect of job, rushes into the boss's office shouting, "Either you do something about this situation or I quit!" Since no one appreciates being faced with a take-it-or-leave-it demand, and even though this employee might be the most valuable and skilled person on the staff, the boss quickly responds, "Don't let the door hit you in the backside when you leave."

Elise became a young widow when her son Zack was nine years old. She told him often that he was now the man of the house and gave him many responsibilities that would have been handled by her husband had he been there. Elise even included Zack in many of the decisions she had to make regarding finances, insurance, and major purchases.

Zack grew into a strong six-foot-five-inch, three-hundred-pound, tough young man whom Elise could no longer control. Against her wishes, Zack dropped out of high school in his junior year and apprenticed himself to an electrician so he could make some "real money." He bought a fancy sports car and began to bring young women home. Often Zack would ask his mother to cook a meal for him and his girlfriend and then vacate the house, so he and the girlfriend could use her bedroom. Elise always did as Zack asked.

When Elise's friends found out what was going on, they advised her to throw her son out. "I can't do that," Elise cried, "He's all the family I've got." Then her friends told her she had to stand up to him. Tell Zack that this is no way to treat his mother. "I can't stand up to him," Elise explained. "I'm really afraid of him. Not only is he very big, but, when crossed, he has quite a temper." Elise was feeling more and more angry and depressed about her situation by the day. She knew she had to do something to turn things around. I need some kind of leverage, she thought.

One of Zack's responsibilities was to mow the lawn. Whenever Elise asked him to take care of the lawn, or any other household chore, for that matter, he would either make some excuse or refuse outright to do it. One day, Elise was outside mowing her lawn in the hot sun. Her anger was overwhelming. Then she had an epiphany.

Zack's favorite food was peanut butter and jelly sandwiches. He would always have one with breakfast, take at least two of them with him to work for lunch, and as soon as he came in the door at the end of the day he would fix himself another. If he spent the evening at home, he would fix himself yet another one before going off to bed. Being the dedicated mother that she was, Elise always made sure that her kitchen was well stocked with Zack's favorite brand of peanut butter, his preferred flavor of jam, and his favorite multigrain bread. That evening when Zack walked through the door, Elise was ready with a Level IV Script.

Describe: Although it is your responsibility to mow the lawn, you rarely do it.

Express: That makes me very angry, because I do everything you ask, even things that would be considered way out of line for a mother to do for her son.

Specify: I want you to mow the lawn tomorrow morning.

Neg Con: If you continue to neglect your responsibilities, I will stop supplying the house with peanut butter and jelly.

The following morning, Elise awoke to the sound of the lawn mower cutting the grass.

Scripting   Levels

Level I Script   **Ends in an open-ended question**

Level II Script   **Ends in positive consequences**

Level III Script   **Ends in a question which prompts the adversary to speak the negative consequences**

Level IV Script   **Ends in negative consequences**

Prepare and practice before you speak. Keep repeating the *specify* line until the person understands your message. Remember that the closer you stay to Level I, the more opportunity you have for discussion, negotiation, and a win-win outcome. The longer you wait to confront the situation, the more likely it is that, because of stress, you will find yourself at Level IV. If you go to Level IV, be prepared to lose.

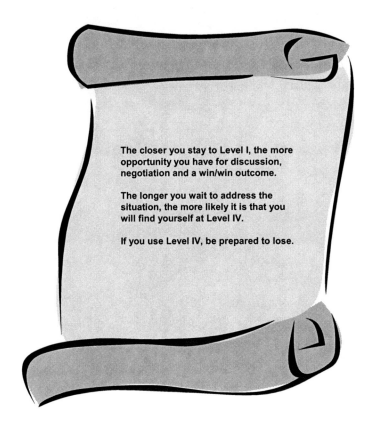

The closer you stay to Level I, the more opportunity you have for discussion, negotiation and a win/win outcome.

The longer you wait to address the situation, the more likely it is that you will find yourself at Level IV.

If you use Level IV, be prepared to lose.

Chapter Ten Exercises

Directions: What follows are some typical situations that generate stress and hostility. Place a checkmark beside the action that you believe would be the best choice to resolve the situation. If you think an assertive script is the answer, use a Level other than Level I as the closing comment. The preferred answers and explanations follow each question on the succeeding pages.

1. You are Patrick O'Riley. Everyone on the staff calls you Pat—except Jack Corbin, who calls you Pattie Yo Ho. You feel this is demeaning, and you really want him to stop it. Your best strategy for dealing with this is:
    *   Ignore the problem.
    *   Confront Jack. Tell him to call you Pat, as everyone else does.
    *   Start calling him Jack-Ass. See how he likes demeaning nicknames.
    *   File a harassment complaint with personnel.
    If your decision is to confront Jack, please design an appropriate script.

    _____

    _____

    _____

    _____

    _____

2. Three months ago, you presented an idea to your boss, which you thought might save the company fifteen hundred dollars per week in administrative costs. Your boss told you it was a ridiculous idea. Your boss then took your idea to the division manager, who immediately implemented it. Your idea has been a great success; it is saving the company eight thousand dollars per week. Your boss is proudly claiming that the idea was his. You want the credit. Your best strategy for dealing with this is:
   - Live with it, and do not give your boss any more good ideas.
   - Put glue on his chair, honey on his keyboard, and black paint on the rear window of his car.
   - Get a voodoo doll of him and stick lots of pins in it; leave it on your desk where he can see it.
   - Go to the division manager and explain what happened; bring any paperwork that supports your accusation.
   - Confront your boss and tell him exactly how you feel. Ask that he make this right by going to the division manager with you to correct the false impression he might have made regarding who developed the idea.

If your decision is to confront your boss, please design an appropriate script.

_____

_____

_____

_____

_____

3. You have recently joined the organization and are about to go on your first travel assignment. Your partner on this trip is an older man who is supposed to show you the ropes. He stops by your office with a big smile and says, "I'm really looking forward

to this opportunity, so we can ... ah (wink) ... get to know each other a little better (wink, wink). I've had my eye on you for some time (really big smile)." Your best strategy for dealing with this is:

- Ask around the office if anyone knows if this guy is gay.
- Tell the boss you want a different partner; refuse to explain why.
- Explain to guy that you have no desire for a personal relationship.
- File a sexual harassment suit with the human resources manager.
- Hang out at the local gay bar and see if he shows up.

If your decision is to explain to the guy, please design an appropriate script.

_____

_____

_____

_____

_____

4. Your brother lives in Chicago, while you and your spouse live in a tiny cottage on the shores of Cape Cod. Five years ago, your brother expressed an interest in visiting you during the summer, so his three boys could enjoy the water. You were delighted to have them come. Now they expect to come every summer for three (terrible) weeks. Your brother's kids are combative, undisciplined, and wild. Last summer, they left their room with one broken floor lamp, one shattered chest of drawers, one busted table lamp, and the cabinet in the bathroom pulled out of the wall. It is now March, and there is a message on your answering machine from your sister-in-law. She wants to discuss the dates for her family's "annual visit to your

quaint little summer cottage." Your best strategy for dealing with this is:

- Send your brother a bill for repairing all the destruction his boys caused; tell him that the bill must be paid before he can visit again.
- Since this is family, suck it up; make the visiting arrangements for the coming summer.
- Inform your sister-in-law that you and your spouse are going to tour Central Asia this summer and will not be home.
- Wipe the call off the answering machine and pretend the call never came in.
- Return the call. Tell your sister-in-law that you are unable to have them visit this summer because of the condition in which the boys left their room last summer.
- Tell your sister-in-law she must keep the boys under control if they visit this summer.

If your decision is to tell your sister-in-law to go elsewhere, please design an appropriate script.

_____

_____

_____

_____

_____

5. Jessie has been a close friend for many years. Over the past several months, you have noticed an alarming increase in Jessie's drinking. You believe the drinking is related to her marital problems. Now you understand that Jessie's drinking has come to the attention of her boss and that Jessie may soon face termination. Your best strategy for dealing with this is:

- Tell Jessie that the grapevine has been spreading the word that she is about to be fired.
- Advise Jessie that others have noticed her drinking problem and that she had better do something about it right away.
- Contact Jessie's spouse and suggest the two of them settle their personal problems before Jessie's drinking gets her fired.
- This is none of your business; stay out of it.
- Tell Jessie that, because of the drinking, you no longer want to spend time with her.
- Risk losing the friendship. Tell Jessie the truth of her situation, and suggest that she seek professional help for her drinking problem.

If your decision is to risk the friendship and tell Jessie the truth of her situation, please design an appropriate script.

---

6. Betsy and Will have been happily married for twenty-five years. Betsy has never had any health issues; Will has had a constant struggle with high blood pressure. He does take drugs to help keep his blood pressure down, but, as he has gotten older, these drugs seem to be less effective. Will's doctor has advised him that he must absolutely stay away from stress-causing situations. In his condition, stress could be fatal. Every year or so, Will's mother Florence comes for a visit. That is the time when his blood pressure goes through the roof. The last time mother visited, Will had to be hospitalized. The doctor said he nearly died. Yesterday, Florence

phoned and announced that she was planning to come for a visit in two weeks. Betsy is frantic; she does not want Will's mother to visit. Will insists that his mother be told nothing about his condition and come for her visit as usual. Betsy's best strategy for dealing with this situation is:

- Go against her husband's wishes; tell Florence she cannot visit and explain why.
- Ask the doctor to phone Florence and explain Will's condition; advise her not to visit.
- Tell the doctor to reserve a room in Intensive Care at the hospital.
- Talk to Will; try again to convince him to discourage his mother from visiting.
- Send Florence tickets for an all-expense paid trip to Hawaii for the same exact dates on which she is planning her visit.
- Since this is family, suck it up; welcome Florence with open arms. Hope for the best.

If your decision is to explain things to Florence, please design an appropriate script.

_____

_____

_____

_____

_____

7. Your teenaged daughter Allison is skinny, tall, flat-chested and rather awkward. She wears thick glasses and sports a mouth full of braces. However, Allison is extremely bright. Unfortunately, she is having a miserable time in high school because she is teased relentlessly by her classmates for being a geek. Last night you found Allison sobbing in her room. Someone had E-mailed her a very

nasty note full of personal insults about her appearance. Allison is angry and depressed. What should you do?

- Suggest that you and Allison take the E-mail to the police as evidence of bullying.
- Tell Allison the story of the Ugly Duckling who grew into a beautiful swan.
- Wrap your arms around her and let her tell you about her anger and frustration.
- Remind Allison that she has a full ride scholarship to MIT while most of her classmates are so dumb they couldn't find their rear ends with both hands and a GPS.
- Explain that her classmates are just jealous of her mental acuity.

If your decision is to say something profound to Allison, please design an appropriate script.

_____

_____

_____

_____

_____

8. Until last year when he was laid off, Robbie had been a thoughtful and loving husband. Although Robbie has worked hard to locate employment, his search has been unsuccessful. Meanwhile, your career has blossomed (good thing since you are now the only wage earner). Robbie has become an argumentative, bitter, combative, critical and all around miserable human being. Nothing you do is right. He yells at you over minor issues and finds fault with you for things you haven't even done yet. You recognize that Robbie is very angry about his situation and is taking out his frustration on you.

You have tried to be understanding but you are sick and tired of being Robbie's whipping boy. What should you do?

- See a lawyer and start divorce proceedings.
- Stand up to Robbie; tell him his treatment of you must change.
- Suck it up. Once Robbie finds a job, the person you fell in love with will reappear.
- Go live with your parents until Robbie finds work.

If your solution is to stand up to Robbie, please design an appropriate script.

_____

_____

_____

_____

_____

Answers to Chapter Ten Exercises

1. You are Patrick O'Riley. Everyone on the staff calls you Pat. The most effective method for dealing with this situation is to confront Jack, tell him how you feel, and ask him to call you Pat, as everyone else does.

    This is a problem you *cannot* ignore. It is demeaning and it diminishes you as a person. Every time he calls you Pattie Yo Ho you will grind your teeth and envision yourself killing him in some manner. Moreover, the more times others on the staff hear this epithet, the more likely it is that they will start using it, too. Calling him Jack-Ass could make you a target of a harassment complaint, because that is insulting. If you file a harassment complaint against Jack without speaking to him first, you will cause ill will and maybe a desire for reprisal.

    Here is an appropriate script:

Describe:	Jack, often, in an effort to be humorous, you call me "Patty Yo Ho."
Express:	This makes me feel uncomfortable, because it's demeaning and unprofessional.
Specify:	I would appreciate it if you would call me Pat, as everyone else does.
Pos Con:	If you do that, it will reflect better on both of us as professionals.

2. Three months ago, you presented an idea to your boss. Your best approach for dealing with this problem is to confront your boss and tell him exactly how you feel. None of the other alternatives will

solve the problem. Some of them will put you in a very bad light, jeopardizing your career. Talking with the boss may not resolve the issue either, but at least you will have stood up for yourself, and you can bet this boss will never do that to you again.

Here is an appropriate script:

Describe: Boss, three months ago I presented you with an idea that has saved the company eight thousand dollars per month in administrative costs.

Express: It makes me feel angry that you have proclaimed the idea as your own.

Specify: I would appreciate it if you would tell the division manager the truth—that the idea was mine, not yours.

Rethink: What do you think is likely to occur to my motivation and loyalty should this fabrication continue?

3. You have recently joined the organization and are about to go on a trip.

    The best answer is to explain to your trip mate that you have no desire for a personal relationship. The man didn't actually say anything that could be interpreted as harassment. It was all done through insinuation and body language cues. He could always allege that you were mistaken. In a one-on-one conversation, you could always say sorry. In any case, your message would have been delivered. Once you bring human resources into the situation, it gets messy. Asking your boss for a different travel partner is a good alternative. However, chances are your boss will insist on knowing why. Moreover, this avenue of resolution will not stop the gentleman's advances. Here is an appropriate script:

Describe: Wayne, from your conversation yesterday, I gathered that you are considering our business trip as an opportunity to develop a personal relationship.

Express:	This made me feel uncomfortable, because I have no interest in doing that.
Specify:	I want us to focus only on business during this trip.
Pos Con:	If we do that, I will look forward to working with you.

4. In return for your gracious hospitality, your nephews are terrorizing you. Certainly your sister-in-law is fully aware of what has gone on, and she has not suggested paying you for the damage, nor has she acknowledged it in any way. Even though this is family, you should stop being a patsy. Call her back and tell her that this summer she and her family will have to make other arrangements because of what happened last summer.

Describe:	Sally, last summer your boys did a good deal of damage to our house during your visit.
Express:	It made me feel angry that you didn't acknowledge the destruction, attempt to stop it, or offer to pay for it.
Specify:	I want you to make your summer vacation arrangements elsewhere.
Pos Con:	Perhaps when the boys are older and more responsible we can consider having you and your family visit us again.

5. Here you have to consider just how strong a friendship you actually have. As a good friend, you should risk the friendship to tell Jessie what you know, see and have observed and let Jessie make the decision about both your friendship and her drinking.

Describe:	Jessie, over the last several months I have noticed a great increase in your liquor consumption. I have also noticed it affecting your work.
Express:	This makes me feel sad and anxious, because I'm certain others have noticed it, too.

Specify: I would like you to seek professional help before things get out of hand.

Rethink: What do you suppose is likely to occur if the boss or a client notices your condition and makes a complaint?

6. Family issues are the most difficult of all. Betsy can beg Will all she wants. Her pleas will fall on deaf ears. After all, this is his mother. His blood pressure soars because he feels trapped: he's a bad son if he tells Mother not to visit and a bad husband if he knowingly puts his life in jeopardy. Betsy's best solution here is to go against Will's wishes and tell Mother Florence exactly what's going on.

Describe: Mother, Will is having a rough time getting his blood pressure under control right now, so it is probably not a good time for you to visit.

Express: This makes me feel both frustrated and anxious, because, although we'd both like very much to see you, the doctor says that any excitement right now might be fatal.

Specify: I would appreciate it if you would put off your visit for a few months.

Pos Con: When the doctor tells us Will's blood pressure is under control, we will happily welcome you with open arms.

7. The best thing you can do is to hold Allison in your arms and let her talk out her anger and frustrations. Allison is ripe for her anger to become depression and depression is a dangerous emotion in a teenager. Allison wants to be accepted by her classmates, included, and liked. That is never going to happen. Even though you will get her contact lenses, the braces will come off and she will wear padded bras, it is her brilliant mind that sets her apart.

One of the greatest tragedies in our schools is how the less intelligent kids treat those who are so very much smarter. People rarely understand intelligence greater then their own anyway. With kids this lack of understanding quickly becomes something close to fear that the more intelligent child is attempting to put something over on them. Allison will face this all of her life unless she finds an environment where everyone is as bright as she is. Getting Allison into action is the best remedy. Here is a script that might make her feel a little less depressed.

Describe:	Allison, what you have received is a very cruel note from a classmate.
Express:	It makes me feel angry that you want to be accepted by such cruel individuals.
Specify:	I want you to take some positive action regarding this miserable note.
Pos. Con:	If you do that, you will feel much better.

8. Your best choice here is to stand up to Robbie. He must realize that although you have tried to be understanding, you have had enough of his abuse. You are drawing a line in the sand regarding his unwarranted aggressive behavior.

Describe:	Robbie, since your layoff, I have noticed a big change in your attitude toward me from positive to negative
Express:	This makes me feel sad and uncomfortable because I am not your enemy.
Specify:	I want us to relate to one another the way we did before you lost your job.
Rethink:	What do you suppose is likely to happen if you continue to work out your anger on me?

Chapter Eleven

Dealing with Criticism

CONSTRUCTIVE CRITICISM, A STANDARD COMPONENT in human interactions, generates a lot of undue anxiety for both the giver and the receiver. Even if the giver offers his or her assessment objectively and with kind understanding, the criticism is seldom well received. A sensitive person knows that pointing out another's deficiencies can be threatening to the receiver's self-esteem, and, in turn, damaging to their relationship. In fact, based on the general reaction to criticism, it is safe to conclude that there is actually no such thing as *constructive* criticism. It is all *destructive*.

There are two kinds of criticism. The first type of criticism is designed to draw your attention to something the other person believes is being handled in an ineffective manner. It is called *valid criticism*, because, in the other person's eyes, it is legitimate, constructive, and justified. It is, however, just the other person's opinion.

The second type of criticism is unfounded criticism; it has no basis in truth. It is often referred to as *manipulative criticism*, because it is designed by the critic purposely to make the other person extremely angry, guilty, or totally demoralized. Here is an illustration of the difference between these two forms of criticism.

Let's suppose you have just given your boss a report that has taken a week of hard work to put together. Your boss could say, "Barbara, I've read over your report. I am concerned about the lack of consistency between the research you utilized and the conclusions you drew from those studies. Please rework that last section of the report so that your conclusions and the research support one another. If you need to, utilize different research sources."

Suppose, however, that your boss wanted to make you feel dumb and inept. He might say, "What the devil is the matter with you, anyway? Can't you do anything right? When are you going to learn that slipshod is not the way we do things around here?"

If the boss wanted you to feel guilty (also a form of manipulative criticism), he might say, "Barbara, I'm really disappointed in you. Every time I give you an important assignment, you let me down and you let the department down."

In the first instance, you know exactly what is troubling the boss about your work, and you also know what needs to be done to fix it. In the second and third instances, not only do you have no idea what's wrong, you are left feeling disrespected, angry, and/or guilty.

Criticism in a close relationship, such as marriage, should be handled with extreme diplomacy, because, no matter how gently it's delivered, there's always the opportunity for hurt feelings.

She: How do you like this new recipe?
He: It's okay.
She: Just okay? Are you saying you don't like it?
He: No, not at all. It's really very good.
She: I hear a *but* in there somewhere. What's wrong with it?
He: Well, nothing really. It's just—I think it could do with a little less salt.
She: So, you think it's too salty.
He: Just a little.
She: Anything else?
He: No.

She:	Are you sure?
He:	Yes, just a little too salty. Otherwise, it's really very good.
She:	Should I make it again?
He:	Yes, but not for guests.
She:	Then you really don't like it.
He:	Not all that much.

The Truth About Constructive Criticism

1. Criticism is not a motivational technique;
   it is designed to focus your awareness on something the
   other person deems to be of importance.

2. Criticism does not teach or show you how to correct
   or change anything.

3. You cannot correct or change something unless you fully
   understand what the problem is and the effect it is having.

4. The other person's perception of the issue is their reality.

Dealing with Valid or *Constructive* Criticism

For most people, any kind of criticism is a very cruel and distressing experience. When it comes from a boss for whom you believe you are doing absolutely the very best job you know how, it can be very painful. Although you may understand intellectually that the sole purpose of the criticism is to assist you in improving some facet of an existing situation, it does not feel helpful at the moment you hear the words. There are some typical, but unproductive, reactions.

- Respond defensively; justify your actions.
- Argue; insist that the boss's (or other person's) point of view is incorrect.

- Become angry; raise your voice, attempt to frighten the boss (or other person) into backing off or terminating the conversation.
- Ask for specific examples. Then show that each example represents an unusual or unique circumstance.
- Say nothing, but through your body language (arms crossed over chest, angry look, eyes averted your eyes), show that you do not agree.
- Smile and agree immediately; keep nodding your head *yes* in an effort to get the conversation over with as quickly as possible.
- Say nothing while the boss (or other person) is talking, but engage in self-righteous *self talk*, telling yourself that you did the right thing. The other person wasn't there; they don't have all the facts; they really do not understand the situation.

What all these reactions represent is *not listening*. Moreover, these reactions make it uncomfortable for the boss (or other person) to continue providing feedback. In order for the criticism to be helpful, both parties must create an environment that encourages candid communication. What follows are some helpful strategies for you to use when you are on the receiving end of criticism. While your boss (or other person) is speaking

- Do not interrupt—listen.
- Listen without commenting facially or physically.
- Listen for the main ideas; concentrate on the substance of the communication.
- Stifle your anger. Resist becoming defensive.
- Avoid the urge to justify yourself.
- Do not pass the buck by blaming others or the organization.

- If you do not understand what is being communicated, say, "Could you say that in another way please?"
- Do not argue with the boss (or the other person); hear him or her out.
- Show receptiveness by expressing interest in learning more.

Once you feel that you have learned as much as you can about what is bothering the boss (or the other person), then, and only then, should you move on to responding to his criticism. The key to dealing substantively and seriously with another person's criticism is to ask questions. Here is an example.

Mark has been a hard-working, dedicated staff member for three years. He has a file of outstanding performance appraisals to prove it. He wants to be promoted, but somehow the opportunity keeps eluding him. He has been reluctant to address the boss about his lack of career movement. He fears the boss might confront him with some humiliating criticism. He finally decides he must speak to the boss in order to learn, understand, and then remedy whatever his shortcomings are, so that eventually a promotion is possible. Mark decides to open the conversation with a script.

Describe:	Boss, although you have given me excellent performance reports for the past three years, whenever promotional opportunities become available, you choose someone else.
Express:	This makes me feel frustrated, because, if my work is so good, you should be promoting me.
Specify:	I would *like* to be promoted into Brad Stone's job when he retires next month.
Question:	How will you help me to secure Brad's job?

Boss:	Mark, you're still new with us. You haven't yet paid your dues.
Mark:	I don't understand what "you haven't paid your dues" actually means. Can you please explain?
Boss:	I've got people who've been waiting for a promotion longer than you've been working here. They are going to be considered ahead of you.
Mark:	I thought promotion was based on work excellence and emotional maturity rather than on longevity. What is the basis for promotion?
Boss:	Well, you're right, of course. Promotion is based on work excellence and emotional maturity, not on longevity. I'm just saying that there are a few good people ahead of you. Be patient; your time will come.
Mark:	What knowledge, skills, or experience am I lacking which prevent you from considering me as fully qualified right now for a promotional opportunity?
Boss:	Well, none actually. It's just that I think you're not quite ready yet for management responsibilities.
Mark:	What exactly am I missing? What do I need to work on so that I am ready?
Boss:	Remember last month when Huston Catcher botched up that customer requirement?
Mark:	Yes.
Boss:	I thought you handled the client's side of things very well, but your conversation with Huston over his negligence was overly harsh.
Mark:	So I need to work on my human relations a little?
Boss:	It's more than that, Mark. You have a lack of patience when dealing with others, especially when those people are not as bright as you are.

Mark:	You're right. Other people's incompetence does drive me nuts. However, if you give me a few months to work on that, I'm sure I can show you an increased tolerance in that area. Is there anything else I need to work on?
Boss:	Yes, there is. As you well know, our consulting work with overseas clients is increasing. Several months ago, the company made language lessons available to anybody interested in learning Chinese and Russian. Although many of the staff enrolled, you did not. While facility with a foreign language is not a requirement today, it may well be in the future. I was surprised that you did not avail yourself of the opportunity.
Mark:	Let me make sure I understand what you're saying. If I want to be promoted to a position of senior consultant, I should become proficient in a foreign language. This is because you anticipate sending consulting teams overseas to work with clients at their locations.
Boss:	That's the plan. But, once again, that's not the whole picture, Mark. Whenever there are opportunities for learning, training, and so forth, you do not sign up. That disturbs me, because this company needs leaders who are continually learning and growing. It's a tough, competitive market out there, and we need a staff that has not ossified itself into mental obsolescence.
Mark:	Thank you very much for your honest feedback. I really appreciate it. I know it was not easy for you to tell me these things. It wasn't easy for me to hear these things, either. However, unless I understand exactly what my deficiencies are, I can't correct them.
Boss:	I understand. So, now that you know what to work on, what will be your next step?

Mark:	I want to draw up a written plan for confronting both those issues. I would like to meet with you again, say next week, to show you that plan. We can then discuss putting my plan into operation immediately.
Boss:	Sounds good. I have Monday at 3:00 PM available.
Mark:	See you then.

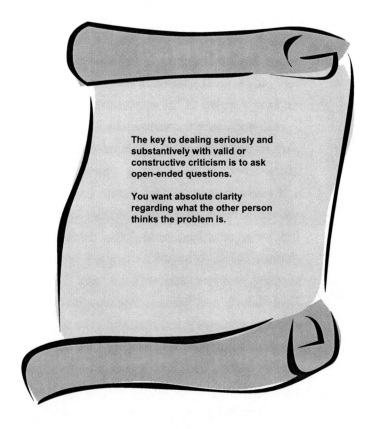

The key to dealing seriously and substantively with valid or constructive criticism is to ask open-ended questions.

You want absolute clarity regarding what the other person thinks the problem is.

The keys for dealing with constructive criticism in a productive manner are listed below.

- Focus your questions on what must be done in the future—*not* what happened in the past.

- Ask questions that provide you with a clear understanding of the boss's (or other person's) terms and the exact meaning of their words and jargon-type phrases.
- Explore the feedback (under what conditions did it occur; when did it occur; what were the perceived negative results; to whom? etc.).
- Summarize your understanding of the problem by saying, "As I understand it, you are concerned about _____ and you would like me to _____. Is that correct?"
- Keep talking and questioning until the boss (or other person) confirms that you fully understand the message.
- Convey appreciation for the feedback.
- If you agree that the boss (or the other person) is correct, say so, and apologize, if appropriate.
- If you believe that the criticism is unwarranted or inaccurate, say so, but only after hearing the boss (or other person) out and fully exploring the situation with him or her.
- If you believe that the criticism *might* be unwarranted or inaccurate, say so, but state that you will think about it.
- Establish some follow-up activity. This is the only way for the boss (or other person) to know that you sincerely value his input.

Let's look in on our pre-divorce couple. Here they engage in mutual criticism, without asking questions that gain a clear understanding of one another's issues. It is the end of the workday and both have arrived home. She is in the kitchen preparing dinner. Without saying a word to her, he enters the kitchen and takes a beer out of the refrigerator. He then goes into the living room, turns on the TV to the evening news, picks up the newspaper and, with a sigh, collapses into his favorite easy chair. How a man can read the newspaper while listening to the television is one of the world's great mysteries, but that is what he's doing. She walks out of the kitchen, hands on her hips, looks at him with his head buried in the newspaper, and bellows "What the hell are you doing sitting there?"

He doesn't understand why she's attacking him with such a stupid question. Nevertheless, he answers her. "What does it look like I'm doing? I'm watching the news."

In response, she stomps over to him, waves her hands about and continues her onslaught. "You are the most inconsiderate person I know."

Instantly angry, he stands up, throws the newspaper on the floor, turns to face her, and yells back. "I've had a tough day at the office and a miserable commute home. I don't need any crap from you!"

Her retort comes quickly. Pulling off her apron, she screams, "You know something? You're impossible. I'm going out. You can fix your own dinner!"

If we replay this little scene using a questioning strategy, the situation does not get into pre-divorce mode.

She:	What the hell are you doing sitting there?
He:	What makes you ask that?
She:	You walked right by me and never said a word. Now you've got your head buried in the sports section with the TV blaring. What the hell's the matter with you anyway? What am I, a piece of wallpaper?
He:	I didn't mean to ignore you, honey. I've had a tough day at the office and a miserable commute home. I just wanted a few minutes of peace and quiet to chill out. What do you want me to do? Would you like some help in the kitchen?
She:	No, but you could at least come in here and talk with me.

He: I have a better idea. Why don't you grab yourself a beer and come into the living room with me and relax for a few minutes. Dinner can wait.

At work, there is a formal occasion set aside for criticism—the performance feedback tête-à-tête. This is a total misuse of what should be a coaching session focused on strengthening a person's career competence. The key to a positive appraisal session is preparation, especially if it is *your* performance appraisal. Prepare yourself for the feedback dialogue. Anticipate any possible criticism so that you will be better able to react to it positively and with a degree of emotional maturity. Here are some ideas for preparing yourself for a performance discussion.

- Know your own strengths and weaknesses.
- Know your boss's expectations for your performance with excruciating clarity.
- Know what is important to your boss (she's compulsive about time, a neatness freak, obsessive about responding quickly to clients, etc.).
- Do some self-evaluation. Measure the degree of success and failure of any task or project in which you are involved. Be prepared. Do not wait to hear the bad news from someone else.
- Discriminate between truth, wishful thinking, and hard facts regarding your performance.

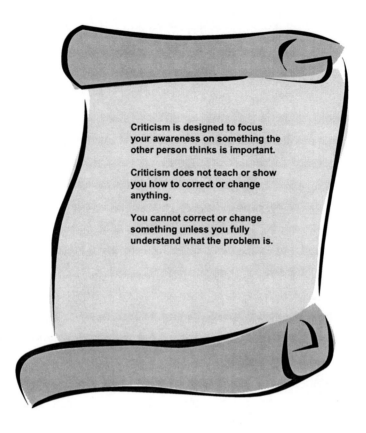

> Criticism is designed to focus your awareness on something the other person thinks is important.
>
> Criticism does not teach or show you how to correct or change anything.
>
> You cannot correct or change something unless you fully understand what the problem is.

You might be interested in knowing that on every performance feedback form there is always a place for the manager to write something about a person's ability to handle criticism. When managers at all levels were asked to define what they meant by the term *ability to handle criticism*, everyone stated that it meant:

- The employee listened and did not argue about what the manager said.
- The employee immediately did whatever the manager suggested.

Dealing with Manipulative Criticism

The second type of criticism—*manipulative* criticism—is the most difficult of all to handle. Perhaps this is because its manipulative quality induces an almost uncontrollable and irrational rage response. Manipulative criticism is unjustified criticism. Its only purpose is to hit your hot buttons, so that you either

- feel guilty
- feel angry, or
- feel out of control

It is a method which places control of your behavior in the hands of the other person. Learning to recognize and respond to manipulation without allowing it to arouse your feelings of anger or guilt is truly an accomplishment. It is a triumph of emotional maturity and human relations insight.

Countermeasures to Manipulation

The Truth	The Manipulation	The Response
#1 You have the right to judge your own behavior.	The *shoulds*; arbitrary rules or structure imposed by others	"I understand what you think but I'm still going to..."
#2 You have the right to offer no reasons to justify your behavior.	Questions beginning with "Why don't you" requiring explanations	"Because I do (or don't) and that's the way I feel ..."
#3 You have the right to judge whether you are responsible for other people's problems.	The well-being of others should come ahead of your comfort	Restate your intent.
#4 You have the right to change your mind.	Only irresponsible people change their minds	Restate your intent.
#5 You have the right to make mistakes.	Good people don't make mistakes so atonement is required	Admit your mistake; do not apologize.
#6 You have the right to say "I don't know".	"What would happen if everyone.."	"I don't know. What would happen?"
#7 You have the right to be independent of the goodwill of others	Without conformity and the goodwill of others, you can't survive	Don't seek affection from others by disrespecting yourself. Do what you think is right.
#8. You have the right to be illogical in making decisions	Logic makes better decisions than you can	Logic is what other people use to prove you wrong
#9. You have the right to say, "I don't understand."	If people have to spell things out for you, you're insensitive; you *should know*...	"How can I know if you don't tell me?" Respond to the words, not the insinuation
#10. You have the right to say, "I don't care"	You must strive to be perfect; constructive criticism is for your own good.	"I understand what you're saying, but I really don't care to ..."

Conventional wisdom insists that in order for us to survive successfully, it is necessary for others to like us. If you believe in this myth, then you become easy prey for manipulation. In order to secure the approval of others, you might agree to do things that are not in your own best interests but are rather what others want you to do. As a result, you feel aggravated when you do what *others* want and guilty if you do what *you* want to do.

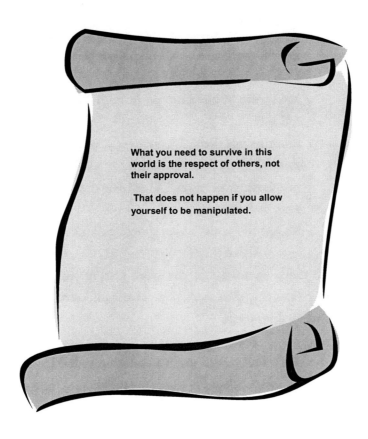

What you need to survive in this world is the respect of others, not their approval.

That does not happen if you allow yourself to be manipulated.

It is easy to see that manipulative criticism is an aggressive act. Our experience of it is that we are being attacked. What is not so easy to see is that guilt-inducing comments are also an aggressive form of criticism. In fact, manipulation through guilt gets us to beat up on ourselves. It is a time-honored method that mothers are apt to use.

Mom:	How come you never call?
You:	Mom, I'm on the phone right now.
Mom:	Your brother John calls me every day.
You:	Gee whiz, Mom, my job requires me to travel into different time zones, and it's not always convenient to call you. I call when I can.
Mom:	If you were really concerned about me, you'd call much more often. You know, I might not be here much longer, with my condition and all.
You:	Mom, the phone lines go in both directions. You can call me.
Mom:	If you're not there, I have to talk to a machine? A fine thing! It's not even human.
You:	Just leave a message. I'll call you right back—well, as soon as I can.
Mom:	It's not the same. A son should call his mother.

There are many occasions in the work setting for manipulation through guilt. Take this next exchange, which undoubtedly you have experienced more than once.

Stan:	We'd like you to make a donation to the United Way.
You:	Thank you, but I'm not interested in making a donation at this time.
Stan:	Do you realize that you're the only person in the department who hasn't made a contribution?
You:	I wasn't aware of that, and I'm still not interested in making a donation at this time.
Stan:	But this is money to help people who cannot help themselves. Don't you care about the poor, the handicapped, and the homeless?

You:	I do care about those people, but I'm not interested in making a donation at this time.
Stan:	Everyone in the department will be aware of your lack of generosity. You are going to be very embarrassed.
You:	I'm still not interested in making a donation at this time.
Stan:	Without your contribution, we're going to be the only department that doesn't reach 100 percent participation. And it will be because of you. How can you do that to us?
You:	I'm sorry about that, but I am still not interested in making a donation at this time.
Stan:	You know, you are letting everyone down in the department. All of us were counting on your participation.
You:	Sorry about that. I'm still not interested in making a donation.
Stan:	You don't have to give a lot; a few dollars will do just fine. Surely you can afford to give two dollars.
You:	Let me put it to you this way: *I—am—not—interested—in—making—a—donation!*
Stan:	Not even two dollars?
You:	No.
Stan:	Will you at least think about it?
You:	In the unlikely event I change my mind, I'll let you know. In the meantime, I would appreciate it if you did not ask me again.

The design of the manipulation is to make you feel so bad that the only way to relieve your guilt is to donate the money. The strategy for dealing with guilt-inducing, manipulative criticism is to stick to your guns, repeating over and over what it is you want or don't want to do.

Now, suppose in the above situation you had responded by making excuses, defending, or rationalizing your decision. You would quickly exhaust your energy and waste your time. Moreover, the entire process will be destructive to your self-esteem. Here's an example of how that conversation might sound.

The Problem with Explanations, Reasons and/or Excuses

- **No one is actually interested in hearing excuses;**

- **Making excuses, explanations, etc. puts you in a defensive stance which is a weak position;**

- **Excuses and explanations give the critic more data with which to open new topics for continuing his/her litany of criticisms.**

Stan:	We'd like you to make a donation to the United Way.
You:	Sorry. I can't right now. I'm really short of funds this month.
Stan:	It's not like I'm asking you for a thousand dollars, for God's sake. All you have to give is a few bucks. Surely you can do that.
You:	You don't understand. My car is scheduled for service this week, Billy's orthodontist needs a payment next week, and my homeowner's insurance is due this month.

Stan:	Why can't you put off servicing the car for another few weeks? I mean, this is really important. You'll be helping those who cannot help themselves.
You:	I cannot put off the car service another time. I've already put it off twice before.
Stan:	How about giving the orthodontist a partial payment? I'm sure he won't mind. Most medical people are pretty understanding and flexible. As long as you pay something, I'm sure it will be okay. What about it? Without your contribution, we're going to be the only department that doesn't reach 100 percent participation.
You:	Well, maybe you're right. I'll call the orthodontist and see if he's willing to take a little less this month.
Stan:	Great! I'll stop by tomorrow for your donation.
You:	(sigh) Yeah, see ya.'

To defend yourself against unfounded or manipulative guilt-inducing criticism, stand your ground by repeating over and over what you want or don't want to do. Avoid conversations or explanation and justification. Not only does that strategy leave you sounding weak, it provides the critic with much too much information with which to continue the manipulation.

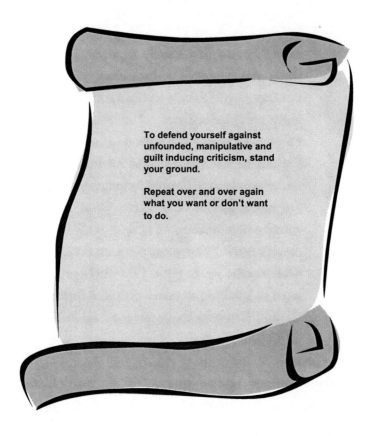

To defend yourself against unfounded, manipulative and guilt inducing criticism, stand your ground.

Repeat over and over again what you want or don't want to do.

The Technique of Fogging

Fogging is used in situations where the manipulative criticism is so outrageous that any conversation at all would be pointless. Fogging deflects the unfounded criticism by responding to the critic's words and not to his or her insinuations. The strategy prevents any confrontation, by making the critic give up his or her verbal attack and go away. This is because you have offered the critic nothing on which he or she can build further comments. Fogging actually stonewalls the critic. Here is an example.

Critic: How can you work with such a messy desk?

You: You're right. It is a mess.

Critic:	Don't you make a lot of mistakes because you're so disorganized?
You:	Why do you ask?
Critic:	I couldn't work that way.
You:	I see.
Critic:	Hasn't the boss spoken to you about this?
You:	I don't understand the question.
Critic:	Organization is one of the boss's pet peeves.
You:	Right!

Fogging is appropriate for petty comments, nosy peers, and stupid questions. It is used when you do not wish to deal with the criticism, but it does *not* solve any problems. Should you wish to deal substantively with the issue, you will ask questions to get additional data for problem-solving. The questioning technique will be illustrated further on.

The fogging technique uses such simple comments as:

"Yes."
"Perhaps you're right."
"Thank you."
"Right."
"I see."
"I know."
"I hear you."
"I understand."

Sara:	That's the same ill-fitting outfit you wore yesterday.
Lisa:	Right; it's the same one.
Sara:	You don't spend a lot of money on your appearance, do you?
Lisa:	You're right, I don't spend a lot.
Sara:	Most of your clothes are out of date, you know.

Lisa:	I know.
Sara:	Surely you must realize that the way you dress doesn't do much for your image as a professional.
Lisa:	I see.
Sara:	Listen, I'm just trying to be helpful. Not everyone would be this honest with you.
Lisa:	Thank you.

Here is another example. Notice that although the critic is attempting to draw the other person into an argument, the target of the criticism refuses to take the bait. Moreover, those fogging responses give the critic absolutely nothing to work with.

Don:	That was some disorganized presentation you made this morning.
Marty:	Perhaps you're right.
Don:	It certainly wasn't up to your usual standard.
Marty:	I hear you.
Don:	I had a tough time making sense of all that gibberish, and I'm sure everyone else did too.
Marty:	I see.
Don:	I wouldn't dare make a presentation like that, especially with all the department heads sitting in.
Marty:	I understand.
Don:	You're not taking me seriously, are you? Just because I'm not your boss doesn't mean my observations aren't valid, you know.
Marty:	I know.

Sometimes the unfounded criticism will take the form of an illogical matching of cause and effect. What the critic actually does is tie two unrelated things together in the form of a criticism. What you do is:

- Separate the two issues.
- Respond to each issue separately but in the same sentence.
- Use *and* as the dividing word.

Here are a few examples illustrating how to respond to this type of unfounded criticism.

Spouse: If you were more responsible, you wouldn't be such a spendthrift.

Spouse: I am responsible, *and* I do tend to spend more money during the holiday season.

Critic   If you weren't so inconsiderate, you'd have noticed that I needed help yesterday.

You: I am a considerate person, *and* I am not a mind-reader. If you wanted my help, you should have asked for it.

Critic: If you were a decent manager, you wouldn't have your staff working overtime to complete their work.

You: I am an excellent manager, *and* it is not possible for my staff to complete their responsibilities without putting in some overtime.

Critic: If you were a good parent, you would spend more time with the children

You: I am a good parent, *and* I am not able to spend more time with the children.

Another popular form of unfounded manipulative criticism is the exaggerated statement. Here the technique is to repeat the exaggeration, which forces the critic to revise their original statement. Then you respond by saying, "I see."

Critic: How come you're *never* on time for staff meetings?
You: I'm *never* on time for staff meetings?
Critic: Well, you were late yesterday.
You: Oh, I see.

Critic: Do you realize that you're *always* the very last person to submit your travel expenses?
You: I'm *always* the last person to submit my travel expenses?
Critic: Well, you were the last one this month.
You: Oh, I see.

Critic: I must have called you at least *twenty times* last night, and you weren't there.
You: You called me *twenty times* last night?
Critic: Well, it was at least three times.
You: Oh, I see.

Spouse: Must you *always* serve meatloaf when my parents visit?
Spouse: I *always* prepare meatloaf when your parents visit?
Spouse: Well, it sure seems that way.
Spouse: Oh, I see.

It is possible to put several of these strategies together when facing a situation in which you really do not wish to get involved in a lengthy rationalization of your decision.

Neighbor: I see you had another large barbecue party last weekend.
You: Yes, we did.
Neighbor: You neglected to invite us.
You: You're right; we did not invite you.

Neighbor:	You must have had at least ten patio parties this summer, and you didn't have us to a single one.
You:	Ten patio parties?
Neighbor:	Well, maybe not ten, but there were sure a lot of them.
You:	I see.
Neighbor:	So how come you never invite us to your barbecues?
You:	You're right. I have never invited you to our barbecues.
Neighbor:	If you were a good neighbor, you'd have invited us to one or two.
You:	I am a good neighbor, *and* I didn't ask you over.
Neighbor:	I'll bet it's because you think we drink too much and we might embarrass you in front of your precious friends.
You:	Perhaps you're right.
Neighbor:	If Chuck and I had a party, we'd sure invite you.
You:	Thank you.

The Many Forms of Manipulative *Criticism*

Criticism through guilt
The Informational Question
It's wrong to change your mind
It's wrong to be different
Blowing things out of proportion
Tying two unrelated things together
Beating a dead horse

Another method of manipulative criticism is known as *beating a dead horse*. Here the manipulator keeps up a steady recitation describing some mistake the other person has made. No amount of apology or explanation stops the barrage. The intent is not to solve any problem, but, rather, to make the other person feel terrible. Here is an example.

Ben:	You left the light on in the bedroom.
Kay:	I did? Sorry. I must have forgotten to turn it off.
Ben:	You know how important it is to turn the lights off when you leave a room.
Kay:	I said I forgot.
Ben:	Not turning the lights off wastes electricity and gives us a huge electric bill.
Kay:	I know, but sometimes when I'm in a hurry, I forget.
Ben:	Well, you shouldn't forget. Wasting electricity is a serious matter.
Kay:	Yes, it is. I'll try to remember to turn out the lights when I leave a room.
Ben:	When the electric bill comes next month, I don't want to hear you complain about it.
Kay:	Ben, it was a momentary lapse. I forgot. I had my mind on other things.
Ben:	You should not have left the light on in the bedroom.
Kay:	Oh, for heavens sake, Ben, will you please let it go!
Ben:	I would if you'd be a little more responsible about turning off unneeded lights.
Kay:	I said I forgot. Stop making such a big deal out of it.
Ben:	You often forget to turn out lights when you leave a room. It's a bad habit.
Kay:	I understand. I will make a real effort to turn out lights when I leave a room.
Ben:	I bet we'll be having the same discussion again because you'll forget again.
Kay:	You make it sound as if I've committed some great, awful sin.

Ben:	It is critical that you avoid wasting electricity.
Kay:	I said I will try to be more careful.
Ben:	How will you do that?
Kay:	Leave it alone already!

By far the most popular form of unfounded, manipulative criticism is known as the *informational question*. The words sound as if the critic wants information. However, the real message of criticism is hidden behind a question. Often, there is no way to answer such questions except to make a joke out of it. Here are a few examples.

| Critic: | How come you're so stupid? |
| You: | I work at it. |

| Critic: | When are you going to start doing something right? |
| You: | Next Thursday at 2:00 PM. |

| Critic: | What kind of a nut are you anyway? |
| You: | I'm a cashew. |

| Critic: | Where did you get your driver's license, in a five-and-dime? |
| You: | Actually I got it at Wal-Mart. |

If you suspect that someone has asked you a manipulative informational question, the best strategy is to respond by asking the critic a question or by stating outright that you do not understand what they are trying to say. The following words and phrases are very helpful in accomplishing this.

- Why do you ask?
- I don't understand the question.

- What makes you ask that?
- Why do you want to know?
- Do you have a need to know?

Here are a few examples of how this strategy works.

Critic: You think you're better than everyone else, don't you?
You: I don't understand the question.

Critic: What makes you think you have all the answers?
You: Why do you ask?

Critic: What makes you think I'm so stupid?
You: Why do you want to know?

Critic: How come you're so unprofessional?
You: What makes you ask that?
Critic: Well, every time you leave for lunch, you neglect to assign someone to handle your phone. It rings and rings until one of us—usually me—has to answer it. Do you think that's fair?
You: I don't understand the question.
Critic: If you don't designate someone to take your phone calls, everyone assumes you're here, and so your phone rings and rings. It disturbs the entire department.
You: I see.
Critic: Why must you be so inconsiderate of other people's time?
You: I don't understand the question.
Critic: You really don't care that your phone disturbs me all the time, do you?
You: Perhaps you're right.

Critic:	We're all supposed to be on the same team, helping one another. A ringing phone is not helpful.
You:	Right!

In the previous example, although the criticism has been deflected, but there is really no problem-solving taking place. In fact, the exchange may have made the other person very angry. If problem-solving were the goal of that conversation, once the critic said, "You should designate someone to take your phone calls when you are going to be out of the office," the response should have been something like, "That's a good idea. Since I don't have an assistant or co-worker nearby, whom do you recommend I ask?"

Fogging is an excellent technique for use with co-workers who insist on asking totally inappropriate personal questions. You would like to say, "That is none of your business," but those words would be perceived as aggressive. What you want to do is respond in a non-threatening manner but in a way that provides the other person with no information at all.

Nosy:	When are going to have another child?
You:	Why do you ask?
Nosy:	Well, I understand Marsha is pregnant, and you two are such good friends.
You:	I see.
Nosy:	So, are you planning to make an addition to the family?
You:	I don't understand the question.
Nosy:	Oh, I get it. You don't want to tell me.
You:	Right!

Snoopy:	How much did you pay for your house?
You:	Why do you ask?
Snoopy:	I'm just curious. We're going to start looking for a place next month.

You:	Oh, I see.
Snoopy:	So, how much did you pay?
You:	Do you have a need to know?
Snoopy:	Well, since you put it that way, I guess I don't.
Date:	Why don't you want to go to bed with me?
You:	Why do you ask?
Date:	Well, I thought you had a nice time with me.
You:	I did.
Date:	So, why don't you want to go to bed with me tonight?
You:	I don't understand the question.

(Note: It would be wicked to say, "You want a list of reasons?")

You do not have to answer other people's (manipulative) questions.

Suppose criticism is unfounded and manipulative, but you decide to deal with it anyway. You want to get to the root of the problem and resolve it. The best strategy for getting to the truth of things is to ask questions until you have a clear picture of the issue. Do *not* make excuses; do *not* make assumptions; do *not* become defensive. Then, when you think the issue is clear, respond in a professional, confident manner, by asking how the person would like to see the problem or concern resolved. Here are a few examples.

Boss: Why can't you ever get to staff meetings on time?

You: I sense my lateness caused a problem, boss. What difficulty did it cause?

Boss: I was counting on you to collect the status reports from the field personnel and prepare an overview for the management staff, and you weren't here to do it.

You: I'm sorry; I was unavoidably delayed. What can I do to remedy the situation now?

It is important to notice that in the above example, no explanation was given for the lateness. This is because

- Making excuses, rationalizations, and explanations puts you in a weak position.
- Generally speaking, no one is really interested in hearing excuses.
- Excuses and explanations give the critic more data to work with.

Here is the same late-to-the-meeting situation using fogging.

Boss: Why can't you ever get to staff meetings on time?

You: Why do you ask?

Boss:	I was counting on you to collect the status reports from the field personnel and prepare an overview for the management staff, and you weren't here to do it.
You:	Right, I wasn't here.
Boss:	Well, why weren't you here?
You:	I don't understand the question.
Boss:	What do you mean, you don't understand? Where were you?
You:	Why do you ask?

You can see how the fogging responses will not only aggravate the boss, they will not do anything in the direction of solving the problem. Moreover, you might end up having to find yourself other employment.

Asking questions to clarify the situation will generally produce quick results in terms of getting to the real issue. Moreover, it will not frustrate the other person. It is just very difficult to come back with questions when the other person has posed these ambiguous, critical-sounding queries. You quickly become furiously angry (rage), because you recognize that the question is a veiled criticism, one that is probably unjustified. The real issue is, therefore, unclear, so you cannot respond logically. This leaves you feeling under attack, blindsided, and out of control.

Here is one more example of using questions to get the critic to tell you what he or she really means.

Critic:	Why are you so negligent when it comes to the children?
You:	I don't understand the question.
Critic:	You forgot to call the babysitter as I asked, so now we don't have anyone to look after the kids when we go to the theatre.
You:	I clean forgot all about it. What can I do to rectify the situation?

Critic: Well, nothing, really. It's too late to call anyone now. We
             will just have to change our plans to some other night.
You: Perhaps it's not too late. Let me call Phyllis right now.
             Maybe she is still available.

Before moving on to the next chapter, let's look in on our pre-divorce couple. After breakfast and before leaving for work, she asked him if he would please take out the garbage. He agreed, but then he ran a little late, so he left the garbage sitting in the middle of the kitchen floor. It was a very warm day, and, by evening, the kitchen smelled exceptionally ripe. He arrived home first, changed his clothes, and collapsed into his favorite easy chair. She arrived home, took one whiff of that kitchen, and, pointing to the offending bag, shrieked, "What's that doing here?"

He realizes this question is a criticism, and so he hears her question a little differently. What he hears is, "You stupid idiot! I asked you to take out the garbage. You agreed to take out the garbage, but it is still sitting here."

In response, therefore, he hollers back, "So, sue me. I forgot."

She: Are you going senile, or are you just trying to make
             my life more difficult? Do you realize I'll never get the
             stench out of this room?
He: Things would be a lot easier between us if you weren't
             so obsessive-compulsive.
She: Things would be a lot easier between us if you weren't
             such a slob.

Let's replay this using a questioning technique.

She: What's that doing here?
He: I don't understand the question.
She: The garbage.

He:	What about the garbage?
She:	I asked you to take out the garbage. You agreed to take out the garbage, but it's still sitting here.
He:	Oh dear! I forgot all about it. Sorry. I'll take it out right now.
She:	It's a good thing for you that I don't forget to do the food shopping.
He:	(fogging) Right!

What becomes abundantly clear is that most conflicts between individuals occur because one party utilized ambiguous and unclear terminology. The other person interpreted those nebulous terms negatively and critically. Even if the first person meant to suggest something negative, the vagueness of the comment generates an angry reaction in the other person—a reaction which is clearly out of proportion (rage) to what was actually intended. The solution to this communication problem is something many people find exceedingly difficult: to speak clearly, without hints, oblique references, indirect terms, wily words, subtitle nuances, suggestive remarks, or questionable observations.

To illustrate, let's look in on our pre-divorce couple once again. It is late afternoon on a rainy Saturday. She is curled up in a chair, completely lost in a romance novel. He enters the room, hungry, and says, "I guess you don't want any dinner tonight."

What she hears is, "You should be in the kitchen preparing dinner instead of reading that trash. It's time for dinner and I'm hungry. Get moving already!" Therefore, she goes into attack mode and responds, "God forbid I should take a little time for myself. Must I cater to you every minute of the day? If you don't want to wait for me to fix dinner, then go make yourself a PB&J. You're not helpless."

What he hears is, "Go away. You're annoying me. Right now, this book is more important than your stomach." So now he feels justified in going into attack mode as well. "All I did was make a simple statement.

You don't need to go ballistic. You should do something about that quick temper of yours. It's late, and, since you're not in the kitchen, I just assumed you aren't interested in dinner."

If he had just said, "Honey, it's getting on to 6:00 PM. It's time we decide what to do about dinner."

Then she might have responded, "Oh my! I didn't realize how late it was. What would you like for supper?"

Exercises for Chapter Eleven

Directions: One of the most popular forms of criticism comes out in the form of a question. It sounds as if the other person is asking for information, when in actuality he/she is criticizing you. Listed below are twenty questions. Place a checkmark opposite those which you determine are manipulative forms of criticism in the guise of a question.

- Why can't you be more professional?
- When are you planning to go to lunch?
- Why are you looking at me that way?
- How is it that you can never follow my instructions?
- When are you going to start being more considerate of other people?
- When will you be finished with the copier?
- What would happen if everyone wanted a new ergonomic office chair?
- Must you always interrupt me with trivia?
- How come you decided to do the report that way?
- How did you manage to do something so stupid?
- What gave you the idea that I needed a formal report?
- What are you doing about the Bradford issue?
- Did you see what I did with my glasses?
- Well, why didn't you say something about this before?
- Why do you think your response to the customer was not quite adequate?

- What will the neighbors think if they know you were out past midnight?
- Why did he say that to you?
- Why won't you have sex with me?
- How come it's always my fault?
- How come you didn't try to do it by yourself?

Answers to Chapter Eleven Exercises

The following items illustrate the *informational question* form of criticism:

Why can't you be more professional?
How is it that you can never follow my instructions?
When are you going to start being more considerate of other people?
Must you always interrupt me with trivia?
How come you decided to do the report that way?
How did you manage to do something so stupid?
What gave you the idea that I needed a formal report?
Well, why didn't you say something about this before?
What will the neighbors think if they know you were out past midnight?
Why won't you have sex with me?
How come it's always my fault?
How come you didn't try to do it by yourself?

You want to get someone agitated and inflamed quickly? Try a few informational questions on them. Spouses are always doing this to one another. Informational questions are probably the single biggest reason for divorce.

- She says, "Why didn't you replace the toilet paper?"
- He says, "How come we're having chicken again for dinner?"

Chapter Twelve

Dealing With Passive-Aggressive Behavior (Hidden Conflict)

BY THIS TIME, YOU OBVIOUSLY understand that, if you are in a conflict with someone, the best thing to do is go and talk to the person. You want to see if you can reach some sort of resolution with which both of you can live. There are some people, however, who will do anything to avoid an honest confrontation. They attempt to keep their conflict hidden and their anger inside.

The conflict and the anger, however, do not actually remain hidden. The hostility comes out in annoying behaviors, such as forgetting to do important tasks, calling in sick at strategic times, doing exactly what the boss said (in spite of knowing that whatever the boss said was not what the boss meant), making mistakes, and so on.

This type of behavior is called *passive-aggressive*. The *passive* part means the mistakes are common and can be easily explained away as honest errors. The *aggressive* part (rage) means that behind the annoying acts hides a hostile purpose, which is to get even with you for something you did or did not do (and have probably forgotten about long ago). Dealing with passive-aggressive behavior is like trying to nail jelly to the wall. At work, the passive-aggressive person may appear to be just stupid and incompetent. At home, however, a passive-aggressive person can destroy a marriage.

An important part of conflict management is learning to recognize passive-aggressive behavior. Then you must know how to confront it, so that the person is forced to interact with you in a more open and honest manner. Passive-aggressive behavior is a popular strategy, simply because it enables a person to attack you without looking hostile. A person who has some issue with you avoids addressing the issue but acts in ways that are purposefully designed to aggravate you. Your state of exasperation (rage) levels the playing field for her and provides a small sense of satisfaction. Here are a few true stories that illustrate passive-aggressive behavior in action.

Susan was the first female supervisor in a department of six. Whenever the manager held a staff meeting with his supervisors, he would ask her to go get coffee and donuts for everyone. She was furious about this; she found it demeaning. This was a new promotion, and, really, in the scheme of things, getting coffee was a minor issue. So, rather than confront her new boss and tell him how the coffee and donuts routine made her feel, she said nothing. She was, however, seething inside.

One day, this woman brought a small bottle of vinegar to work, and whenever her boss asked her to get coffee, she spilled a little vinegar into the cup. The boss's reaction was to declare at every staff meeting to which Susan had brought the coffee, "Gee, Susan, you make one lousy cup of coffee. Perhaps you should take a cooking lesson in how to make coffee." Although she felt happily justified in what she was doing, her actions did not solve her problem.

Lucas was a very active, handsome man in his early fifties, who enjoyed hunting, fishing, and other outdoor activities. Betty, his wife, was a sweet homemaker type, who preferred to remain at home doing things like sewing, decorating, and cooking. After twenty-five years of marriage, Betty discovered that Lucas was having an affair with one of the neighbors. Instead of speaking with Lucas about it, Betty suddenly developed all kinds of medical issues that not only confined her to the house but forced Lucas to become her caregiver. Doctors could not find anything medically wrong with Betty. Meanwhile, Lucas had to give up all the outdoor activities he loved in order to look after Betty. Finally, a friend suggested that Lucas end his affair to see if that might have a positive affect on Betty's condition. Lucas was embarrassed that friends knew about his infidelity; he was so sure he had been discreet. He decided to take the friend's advice. As soon as he ended the affair, Betty's mysterious medical condition improved.

He was a hard-working international peace negotiator whose travel assignments made up more than 70 percent of his job. His wife was about to deliver twins, so he asked his boss for a reduced travel schedule during her final month. The boss reminded the man that his job included a heavy travel schedule. He had known that when he was hired. The boss made it abundantly clear that she did not care what was going on in his household. The State Department was depending on him to fulfill his travel responsibilities, and she was going to ensure that he did so. In the final month of his wife's pregnancy, the man misplaced his passport. He had to wait three weeks for a new one to be issued. During that time, he was unable to travel, so he was at home for his wife's delivery.

In both these stories, the unreasonable behavior of the *targets* did not change. Moreover, the targets of the passive-aggressive behavior most probably never got the message; they just got irritated. The passive-aggressive person, however, clearly felt justified and happy that he/she had evened the score.

What is perplexing about passive-aggressive behavior is that you might not realize you have angered a person until these strange behaviors start showing up. To stop the behavior from continuing, you must confront the person and keep pushing to get at the reason for the annoying behavior pattern you have identified. In the following example, the manager has to keep pushing and pushing for an explanation of the behavior—and then push again for a solid commitment that it will stop. Eventually the true reason for the annoying behavior comes out, but it takes a very long time.

You are a supervisor who frequently asks a particular employee if she can take on a voluntary task. The employee always agrees, but somehow that task never gets done. Either she forgets to do it, or she loses the paperwork somewhere on her desk, or she waits until the last minute to tell you she just couldn't squeeze it in. This has happened several times.

You:	Lucy, it's time again for the department's action report, and I was wondering if you would once again volunteer to take on the responsibility for putting it together.
Lucy:	Oh, sure, boss. Just leave it on my desk, and I'll get to it when I can.
You:	Look, Lucy. I really appreciate your willingness to take this task off my hands. However, the last four times you agreed to handle this for me, the report somehow didn't get done. Either you forgot to do it, or it was buried on your desk, or you were just too busy to get to it. You really need to be honest with me. If you do not want to do it, I'll just ask someone else. But you need to tell me the truth.
Lucy:	Oh no. That's fine. Just leave it on my desk, and I'll try to get to it.
You:	That doesn't sound like much of a commitment to me. Perhaps we should look at your priorities and see if you can actually squeeze it in. What do you think?
Lucy:	Oh, we don't need to do that. I'll probably be able to get to it.
You:	Probably? I need something more definite from you than "probably."
Lucy:	Well, I'll really try my very, very best to get to it. Really, I will.
You:	Trying your best isn't enough. I need a firm statement from you that if you agree to do the action report, you will have it completed by this Thursday.

Lucy:	I think I can probably get to it. Just put right there on top of that stack (pointing). I will try not to disappoint you this time. You need it by Thursday, did you say?
You:	Yes, by Thursday. Lucy, I want you to be honest with me. It's all right for you to tell me that you don't want to take on any more work. I can always ask someone else.
Lucy:	Well, I really have a lot on my plate right now and ... ahh ...
You:	Yes, I know.
Lucy:	It's just that ... oh, never mind. Just leave the report. I'll try to get to it.
You:	What were you going to say, Lucy? It's important that we be open and honest with one another. Otherwise, both of us will be unhappy.
Lucy:	I really don't understand why I'm always the first person you ask to do these dumb reports. There are six other people in the area you could ask, and not one of them is as busy as I am.
You:	I ask you because you are the most experienced. Moreover, everything you do is of high quality, so I can trust that the report, when done, will be done correctly.
Lucy:	I really hate these compliments that always come before you dump extra work on me. Maybe if I screwed up once in a while, I wouldn't have to work as hard.
You:	Sounds as if you're really angry about doing these reports. Are you?
Lucy:	I'm not really angry. I just feel I'm always being taken advantage of. Then, when raises come around, I get the same as everyone else. It's just not fair.
You:	I get the picture. I will not ask you to do these reports again.
Lucy:	Well, um ... I don't want to disappoint you. I know these reports must be done correctly, and they are

	complicated. Not everyone can do them. (sigh) Just leave them here. I'll try to get them done.
You:	You will disappoint me if you agree to do it and then don't. It is a voluntary assignment. I can always ask someone else to do it.
Lucy:	Is this really a voluntary assignment? I don't have to do it?
You:	You don't have to do it. This task is not a part of your normal responsibilities. It is part of my job. You'll be doing me a big favor if you can take it on.
Lucy:	You won't think I'm uncooperative?
You:	No. Not if you're too busy.
Lucy:	But what's going to happen at performance appraisal time? Will you give me an unsatisfactory rating because I'm unwilling to take on extra assignments? Will you tell me I am not a team player or that I am uncooperative?
You:	Is that why you always volunteer for extra work but rarely follow through by actually doing it?
Lucy:	Well ... ahh ... yes ... I'm tired of being taken advantage of—but I don't want to get an unsatisfactory evaluation because I refused extra work.
You:	This is truly a voluntary task. You can be honest with me. If you cannot guarantee that you can have the report done by Thursday, just say so. I will ask someone else to do it. It's not a big deal, and it will not be a mark against you in any way.
Lucy:	Well ... if you're sure.
You:	Yes, I'm sure. Just be honest with me.
Lucy:	Please ask someone else to do the report. I am really behind in my work right now, and I know I will not be able to get to it.

You:	Thank you for being honest with me. In the future, Lucy, please do not volunteer for extra assignments unless you can honestly promise you will get that assignment done on time.
Lucy:	Okay!
You:	Based on your feedback today, I will make sure that in the future I ask others—not just you—to assist with the extra assignments. You are absolutely right that I should not punish you with extra work just because I can rely on you to do a quality job.
Lucy:	Thank you.

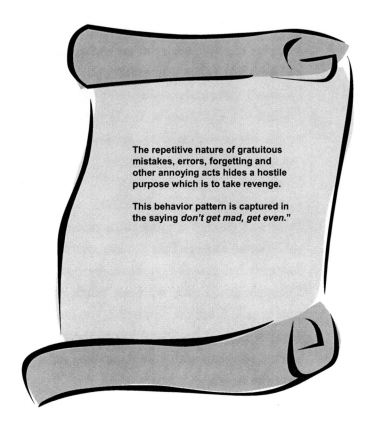

The repetitive nature of gratuitous mistakes, errors, forgetting and other annoying acts hides a hostile purpose which is to take revenge.

This behavior pattern is captured in the saying *don't get mad, get even.*"

Suppose you have a good friend named Murphy at work. Both of you had been considered for the same promotion. You were the successful candidate. Ever since the announcement of your promotion, Murphy has been doing small things that really aggravate you. When you request information from his area, he delays sending it. If he answers your phone while you are away, he forgets to give you the messages. Yesterday, because your car was in the shop, Murphy offered to drive you home. When you stopped by his cubicle at 4:30 PM, he said he was just going to "finish up a few things." Thirty minutes later, the two of you left the office. Then, on the way home, Murphy stopped to get a few items at the grocery store. That took another thirty minutes. Your family was very upset by your lateness and couldn't understand why you had not taken the bus home.

You:	Murphy, can you please tell me the real reason why we left the office so late yesterday?
Murf:	I'm sure I don't know what you're talking about.
You:	I'm sure you do, Murphy. You're always one of the first people out of the building, yet yesterday, you delayed our departure for thirty minutes.
Murf:	I had a few things to finish up.
You:	I think there's more to it than that.
Murf:	I was nice enough to offer you a ride home, and now you're complaining? Take the bus next time.
You:	I actually had planned on taking the bus this time, but I thought that riding with you might give us a little time to talk. Since my promotion, you seem distant and angry with me. Our friendship has become strained. I wanted to speak with you about it to see if we could clear the air.
Murf:	There's nothing to say.

Murf:	But you're angry with me. What did I do to make you so angry that you won't even talk to me about it?
Murf:	You? Nothing. You did nothing.
You:	Then why are you so angry?
Murf:	Will you just forget it and leave me alone?
You:	If we don't discuss it, we'll never solve the problem, and I want our friendship back.
Murf:	You mean you actually want to fraternize with a lowly supervisor?
You:	So you are angry about my promotion.
Murf:	I didn't say that.
You:	Look Murphy, I didn't promote me. The boss did. If you have an issue about that, you need to speak with him. Don't take out your frustrations on me. I don't deserve that.
Murf:	You're right. But I don't understand why he selected you over me. I have more years in than you, I took extra courses at night school, which you didn't. He should have picked me.
You:	I can certainly understand your anger [rage], but you need to speak with him. I didn't have anything to do with the selection process. I was just another name on the list. I went through the exact same interviewing process as you did. Go speak to the boss.
Murf:	You're right. I should speak to him. It's just that I am so angry about this that I might go off the deep end and tell him what I really think.
You:	Nevertheless, Murphy, he is the only person who can explain why he did not select you for the position.
Murf:	I know. I know. Sorry for directing my frustration at you. I'm just very upset.
You:	I understand.

Once again, let's look in on our pre-divorce couple. Since he and she both work, his shirts are always done at the local dry cleaners. Today he is going to an important business meeting. The shirt he wants to wear is a bit wrinkled. He therefore asks her to please give it a little touch-up with the iron. She hates to iron, and he knows it. She places his fine shirt on the ironing board, back side up. She plugs in the iron, dials it to *char,* and leaves it there for ten minutes. When the smoke starts to rise, she takes the shirt to him, shows him the iron-shaped burn mark and, smiling, says, "Here's your shirt—ironed!"

He: What the hell happened?
She: I have to get dressed to go to work too, you know. I just turned my back for a minute. Sorry.

Chapter Twelve Exercises

Directions: In the following situations, *first* identify the passive-aggressive solution. Place an *X* beside it. Then select the solution that you believe will best resolve the situation. Place a checkmark beside it.

1. A co-worker is very upset at something you did. She is yelling at you, using abusive and threatening language. Your best strategy for dealing with this is
    *   Listen patiently, say nothing, and then walk away.
    *   Match the loudness and intensity of her voice. Ask, "How would you like to resolve this?"
    *   Apologize profusely and tell her you're just a doofus.
    *   Put your fingers in your ears and stick your tongue out at her.
    *   Tell her to "Shut the hell up and stop behaving like a child!"

2. Patel Golobamrai sits right beside you at work. He's a hard worker, smart, courteous to a fault, and always willing to help others. The man, however, reeks of curry spice and other exotic cooking smells. It is making you sick. Your best strategy for dealing with this is:
    *   Ask your boss to relocate your work space.
    *   Speak to Patel about the benefits of regular bathing and changing of clothes.
    *   Suggest that Patel use the services of a dry cleaner, and offer to pay his first ninety days of bills.

- Ask Patel to recommend a good Indian restaurant, and eat there several times a week until you get used to the smells.
- Leave a care package of deodorant, men's cologne, breath freshener, and soap on his desk.

3. You have a co-worker who consistently interrupts you. Whether you are talking to him, speaking privately to another person, or making a presentation at a meeting, he interrupts. When this person is around, it is impossible for you to complete a sentence. Your best strategy for dealing with this is:
   - Don't speak when he's in the vicinity.
   - Write an anonymous note saying that his interrupting behavior is angering the entire staff and makes him look unprofessional. Leave the note on his desk.
   - At the next meeting when he interrupts, in front of everyone, shout, "Why don't you put a sock in it, Harry?"
   - Start interrupting him whenever he speaks.
   - E-mail a request for a one-on-one meeting to discuss this issue. Come to the meeting with a sign that says "You're Interrupting Again," which you can hold up whenever he tries to interrupt you.

4. You share an apartment with someone who always manages to worm her way out of paying her fair share of the rental expenses. Since your name is the one on the lease, you have been making all the payments. Your best strategy for dealing with this is:
   - Refuse to pay anything toward the other expenses you both are supposed to share, like food.
   - Advertise for a new roommate. When you find someone you like, ask this one to pack up and get out.
   - Present your roommate with an analysis of exactly what she owes, and ask for the money.

- Look for a new apartment which you can afford by yourself.
- Ask your roommate to pay up or move out immediately.
- Change the locks, and tell the roommate she can have her things when she pays you.

5. Your son pestered you for months to get him a dog. When you finally did get him a dog it was with the understanding that he, not you, would be taking care of it. Lately, your son has come up with all kinds of excuses for **not** being able to walk the dog in the evening. This week, he forgot to feed the dog three times. You have a demanding full time job and cannot take on the added responsibility of a dog. Your best strategy for dealing with this is:
- Take the dog to the pound.
- Have the vet put the dog down.
- Inform your son that you will not feed him, do his laundry or clean his room until he assumes full responsibility for his dog.
- Tell your son that if he chooses to avoid taking responsibility for the dog, he must also choose to give the dog up.
- Advise your son that you do not intend to look after his dog.

6. You have a neighbor whose yard looks like a garbage dump. It is filled with rusted car parts, broken barrels, busted toys, damaged camping equipment, smashed bicycles, old garden pots and assorted corroded tools. You have asked this neighbor to please clean up his yard. You even offered to help him do it. So far, however, nothing has changed. No doubt his junk filled yard is affecting the real estate values of the neighborhood. Your best strategy for dealing with this is:
- See if your neighbors will join you in a legal suit.
- Complain to the Board of Health that your neighbor is causing a health hazard.

- Contact the police department. Ask that they speak to your neighbor.
- Start a fire in the neighbor's yard.
- Call a real estate agent and put his house up for sale at a ridiculously low price.
- Contact a junk dealer and pay him to clean up your neighbor's yard. Then give the neighbor the bill for the cleanup.

Answers to Chapter Twelve Exercises

1. A co-worker is very upset at something you did. She is yelling. The passive-aggressive response is: Listen patiently, say nothing, and then walk away. The best strategy is: match the loudness and intensity of her voice, while asking, "How would you like us to resolve this?"

    None of the other choices will solve the problem. Some will only make your co-worker angrier. The open-ended question will pull her into a problem-solving mode. Matching the loudness and intensity of her words allows you to cut through her tirade quickly.

2. Patel Golobamrai sits right beside you at work. The passive-aggressive response is to leave a care package of deodorant, men's cologne, breath freshener, etc., on his desk. Your best solution is to ask your boss to relocate your work space.

    The other choices might well put you in danger of a discrimination complaint. Eating at an Indian restaurant is a creative attempt at a resolution, but it might not work for you.

3. You have a co-worker who consistently interrupts you. The passive-aggressive solution is to write an anonymous note saying that his interrupting behavior is angering the entire staff. The only alternative that stands a chance of being effective is the last one. E-mail a request for a one-on-one meeting to discuss this issue. Come to the meeting with a sign. This unfortunate behavior is learned at a young age and has something to do with feeling that he has to prove something in every situation. Perhaps he's trying to prove that he's smarter or more dedicated than everyone else.

4. You share an apartment with someone who doesn't pay her fair share. The passive-aggressive approach is to advertise for a new roommate without telling the present roommate you are doing so and why. The best strategy is to present your roommate with an analysis of exactly what she owes and ask for the money. If the roommate pays, your problem is solved. If she refuses, you should probably ask the roommate to move out. Locking up the roommate's possessions might cause legal problems.

5. Your son is not taking care of the dog. The passive-aggressive choice is to either put the dog down or take the dog to the pound. The best strategy is to force your son to make a choice and take responsibility for that choice—to "man-up." Tell your son that if he chooses to avoid taking responsibility for the dog, he must also choose to give up the dog.

6. Your neighbor's yard looks like a dump. The passive-aggressive choice is to put the neighbor's house up for sale—although, in some instances, believe it or not, this has worked. The neighbor took the money and left the area. Since you have already tried talking to this neighbor and had no success, your next best alternative is to contact the police department and ask that they speak to your neighbor.

Chapter Thirteen

Where Anger Comes From

ANGER (RAGE) IS A COMMONPLACE emotion that strikes often in our daily lives. A simple event can be the trigger. Perhaps a co-worker criticizes you in front of others. Maybe it is a person who sneaks into a parking lot space for which you have been waiting.

Immediately you make a mental evaluation of that event, based on whether or not you can manage it effectively. This evaluation has to do with your sense of being in control of the particular situation. If you decide you can handle that situation, that you are in control of things, your anger is not generated. For example, you may decide to just go look for another parking space.

There are folks, however, who would just go ballistic over someone taking their parking space. Such individuals experience a sensation of total loss of control over their own lives. So, immediately, feelings of fear and irrational anger or rage explode inside them.

In the situation of the criticizing co-worker, suppose this happens at a meeting where your boss and several co-workers are present. In such a situation, you are definitely *not* in control. You are presented with the problem of what to do in order to maintain the boss's good opinion of you while looking strong in the eyes of your colleagues. Should you try to defend yourself and deny the charges? How about criticizing the person right back? You feel blindsided, trapped, and muzzled from saying anything. Your fury is almost overwhelming.

ANGER CYCLE

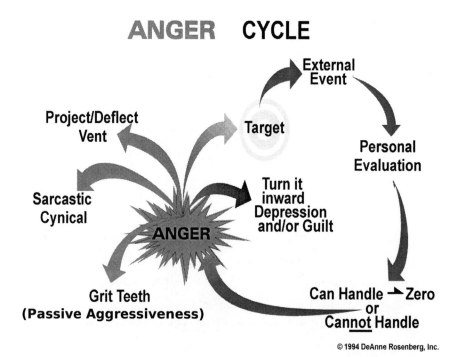

© 1994 DeAnne Rosenberg, Inc.

Perhaps you ask yourself, "Why can't I say something so very clever that my critic will immediately look like a fool?" You are not only angry at the critic, you are also extremely angry with yourself for not being able to deliver a sharp retort. What you would really like to do, probably, is punch the critic right in the chops, because you have been embarrassed and are seriously pissed off.

We learn early on that an outright display of hostility scares others and gives the impression that we are emotionally unstable. However, our daily lives are chock-full of incidents that leave us feeling hostile. The truth of the matter is we all need a way to discharge that hostility. Basically, each of us has only a limited amount of psychological space for holding aggravations inside. Eventually we must unload and vent, or risk becoming psychotic.

Stockpiling anger internally is common. However, each person needs a way to unload some of their accumulated aggression because the psychological space for holding aggravations inside is very limited.

The problem is we never know when somebody has reached their limit and an explosion is imminent.

In our society, there are five typical methods we use to unload our hostility. They are:

1. Turn our hostility and anger inward and blame ourselves and as a result, become depressed.
2. Grit our teeth and bear it; do nothing at the moment; look for an opportunity to get even.
3. Become cynical, sarcastic, and humorously insulting.
4. Project our feelings onto someone or something else (like spouses, kids, or the family dog).
5. Direct our anger directly at the person or situation that generated our anger in the first place.

Here is how the first method—turning your hostility inward—works. Maybe you begin thinking, "Why am I always the first person everyone dumps on when anything goes wrong around here? What a loser they must all think I am. Not even my boss came to my rescue, and I worked so hard on that project."

Should you choose this avenue, you'll become depressed and begin feeling like a victim in your own life. When people become depressed enough, they become very disillusioned and may think of committing suicide. Unfortunately, there are times when people do commit suicide. While some introspection is necessary to determine your role in a conflict, obviously, this is *not* a good method to use when dealing with anger.

Depression is the result of holding a lot of angry feelings inside. Not only is this unhealthy, it is also dangerous. Youngsters who turn out to be serial killers are described by friends and neighbors as such "nice, quiet boys." It is only after the killing spree that we realize how much anger those kids must have been holding inside.

Co-workers who go *postal* are said to have just snapped. Well, all this hostility and acting out didn't just happen out of the blue. You can bet that the situation had been building up for a long time. Then, when the person's internal pressure cooker couldn't hold any more, he/she acted out the anger (rage) by coming to work with a gun and killing people.

Therefore, the next time you are feeling down about some situation, ask yourself, "What am I so angry about?" because that's what's really going on with you. Then, when you get to the answer, ask yourself another question—an action question such as, "What am I going to do about this situation?"

The second method is to grit your teeth and bear it. You do nothing at the moment, but you look for an opportunity to even the score later on. In the work setting, this is the most popular method of conflict management.

For example, an employee may be very angry at his boss because the boss did not recommend him for promotion. The employee then limits his work output, dedication, and productivity as a way of getting even. The employee may feel it is too risky to confront the boss about his dissatisfaction. In reality, however, talking to the boss is the only way to deal effectively with the situation.

Here is another common situation. Mother comes home from the hospital with a new baby. Although she makes many speeches to her five-year-old that she is still number one in the household, the five-year-old can plainly see that all the parents' attention is squarely focused on the baby and not on her at all. So the older child, who had long ago stopped wetting the bed, starts to wet the bed again.

In the parking space situation, the grit-your-teeth-and-get-even-later response might look like this. You park your car in such a way as to block the fellow who stole your space, and then you disappear for several hours. Perhaps you let the air out of his tires. With the criticizing co-worker, maybe you forget to give them some important information, or you give them incorrect information.

The third method—being cynical and sarcastic—is beautifully illustrated by the humor of Don Rickles. Watching him, we sense what an angry person he is, because there is always such a cruel edge to his jokes. Contrast that with someone like Jay Leno. His jokes are all in good fun. Remember the TV program MASH where the actors spent lots of time and energy playing tricks on one another? As observers, we recognized how very angry they were that the US Army had them patching up solders only to have those solders go right back into harm's way.

If you wanted to take the cynical-and-sarcastic approach with the criticizing co-worker, you might tell him or her, "That's a nice suit you're wearing. Too bad they didn't have it in your size." A relative who is jealous of you—at a family gathering and in a loud voice—might say, "Isn't that the same car you were driving ten years ago?"

Method four—project your anger onto someone or something else—might look like this. When you get back to your office after the meeting where your co-worker criticized you, you scream at your administrative person over some minor oversight. In the parking lot situation, you might go over to the Mall Information Desk and give that poor clerk a piece of your mind regarding nervy people who go around stealing other people's parking spaces.

Let's look in on our pre-divorce couple and see what happens when one partner uses the other for "project and deflect." He has had a series of really unpleasant occurrences today. The company canceled the project on which he's been working for the past several months. His boss gave him an unsatisfactory performance appraisal. On his way to work, he got a traffic ticket. Thus, he walks into the house bellowing, "You know what happened to me today?"

She: Why are you yelling at me? What did I do?
He: Don't start with me. I've had a really miserable day.
She: So why take it out on me? If you're going to come home in a lousy mood, maybe you shouldn't come home at all.

By the way, many people use sports for deflecting and projecting their anger. Think of the guy on vacation playing golf. As he's teeing off, he has a major heart attack. Obviously he was thinking of the golf ball as his adversary and, *kaboom*, he blew out his aorta. If you have people who are runners in your office, recall what they are like during a stretch of bad weather when they cannot get out for their daily run. They're wild; the least little thing sets them off.
So, you ask, if I'm not supposed to:
- turn my anger inward
- grit my teeth and bear it now and look for an opportunity to get even later
- be cynical and sarcastic, or
- project my anger onto someone or something else

what should I do? The answer is use the fifth method. Direct your anger directly at the person or situation which generated your hostility in the first place.

It is here that you will find the *assertive script* of invaluable use. For example, you might say to your co-worker, right at the moment of the criticism, "Ben, if you have something negative to say about me or my work, I would prefer that you say it to me in private."

With the parking spot incident, you might put your car in *park*, walk over to the offending person, and say, "Excuse me. Perhaps you didn't notice but I had been waiting for that parking space. My directional signals were flashing my intention. Therefore, I would appreciate it if you would vacate the space so that I might have it." Directing your anger at the person or situation that generated your anger in the first place is the only way to prevent that internal pressure-cooker buildup of hostility.

When you direct your anger, you do not have to do so in a screaming, hostile, out-of-control manner. You can speak calmly and in a straightforward manner. This allows the other person to really hear your words, not just the hostility.

In the parking lot situation, the other driver might not relinquish the space. In fact, he might give you the finger. Nevertheless, you will feel good, because you stood up for yourself. Moreover, you will not be left feeling as if you are deficient in some way, telling the next twenty people you meet about what happened to you in the parking lot.

There was a woman with two teenaged daughters. Every day there would be a screaming argument between mother and daughters about the girls cleaning up their rooms.

Mother:	I want you to clean up your rooms right now!
Girls:	Just close the door, and you won't have to look at it.
Mother:	That's not the point. Your room is in my house. Get up there and take your clothes off the bed and the floor, hang them up, throw away those paper plates from pizza and those empty Coke cans, and get it done before dinner.
Girls:	If our mess doesn't bother us, why should it bother you?
Mother:	Because my hard work paid for those expensive clothes which are now on the floor.

And so it continued day after day after day. Then, one day, probably because the mother was simply too tired to fight, instead of screaming at them to clean their rooms, she made her request in a normal voice. The girls looked at one another and said, "Okay, Mom." They immediately went back upstairs and cleaned up their rooms. The mother was astounded. After dinner she asked her daughters what had made today so different from the months and months of arguments that had produced no cleaning-up results. One of the girls explained, "Well, Mom, I guess we never really heard you before. We got that you were angry. That made us want to leave the house as quickly as possible. Today you didn't sound so upset."

Anger and hostility are commonplace. Everyone, however, needs some way to discharge or unload his or her hostility. There is nothing positive or negative about this process. We simply have only a limited amount of psychological space for holding things inside. The critical question is: what method will you choose to unload your hostility?

The Effectiveness of Unloading Strategies

Hostility at 100%

Hostility at 90%	Turn anger inward, become depressed
Hostility at 75%	Grit teeth and bear it; look to get even
Hostility at 50%	Make cynical, sarcastic remarks
Hostility at 25%	Project/deflect onto something else
Hostility at 0%	Speak directly to the person

When you take a look at the anger cycle, suddenly it becomes easier to understand how it happens that "nice, quiet people" abruptly fly into a rage killing others. After literally eating their anger for some period of time, people reach a breaking point, and, like a pressure cooker, the lid blows off. These nice, quiet people were living lives of quiet desperation, feeling miserable about their situation. Maybe these individuals believed they had been taken advantage of one too many times. Perhaps they felt that no matter what they tried to do, they would still find themselves in a hopeless situation.

Take the famous story of the wife who was continually being beaten up by her husband. This meek and mild woman lit a fire to the mattress on which her abusive, drunken husband was sleeping and burned him to death. She felt she had no other way out.

Remember the young man who killed so many at Virginia Tech? He was a child of war who had been brought up in fear and scarcity. Now he was surrounded by young people who had been brought up in freedom and plenty. He became envious of all those around him, who had so much, while he was living on a shoestring. He believed he too should be living an affluent life and that that life was not available to him. The more he believed such a life was unattainable for him, the angrier he became. (Recall: The other person's perception of the issue is their reality.) After so long at "grit your teeth and bear it," this boy's sanity ruptured, and all people could say was

"He was such a nice, quiet boy. So polite. I simply can't believe ..."
"He kept to himself most of the time. A bit of a loner, you know ..."
"He was withdrawn, distant, and non-communicative ..."
"He seemed depressed most of the time ..."
"He didn't have any friends ..." or "He only had this one friend ..."
"He didn't belong to any particular group; he was an outcast ..."

We need to watch our children and monitor ourselves, remembering that it is not healthy to hold anger inside. Make it legitimate to express, discuss, and communicate anger before it becomes rage. Then, make it possible for people to unload their anger in appropriate ways.

Chapter Thirteen Exercises

Directions: Complete the following statements.

1. There are _____ ways for me to handle my anger and hostility.
2. Those methods are _____.
3. The least effective method for managing my anger and hostility is _____.
4. This is because this method might result in _____.
5. The most effective method for coping with my anger and hostility is _____.
6. The time when my anger and hostility is most likely to be generated is when I feel _____.
7. I must always remember that if someone is screaming angry words at me, and I did nothing to cause that reaction, they are probably using me to _____.
8. Even though I might be furiously angry, when I confront another person, in order to ensure that he/she truly hears my concerns, I must _____.
9. The old saying "That was the straw that broke the camel's back" refers to someone having reached _____.
10. My fourteen-year-old tells me that someone in his class—a nice, quiet, meek, and timid boy—is being bullied by a few of the older students. I should _____.

Answers to Chapter Thirteen Exercises

1. There are **five** ways for me to handle my anger and hostility.
2. Those methods are:
   - turn my anger inward to myself;
   - project and deflect my anger onto someone or something else;
   - grit my teeth and bear it for now, but look for a chance to get even later on;
   - make caustic, sarcastic remarks;
   - direct my anger directly at the person or situation that generated my anger.
3. The least effective method for managing my anger and hostility is: **turn my anger inward to myself.**
4. This is because this method might result in **suicide.**
5. The most effective method for coping with my anger and hostility is: **direct my anger directly at the person or situation that generated my anger.**
6. The time when my anger and hostility is most likely to be generated is when I feel **fearful and/or not in control of my situation.**
7. I must always remember that if someone is screaming angry words at me, and I did nothing to cause that reaction, they are probably using me to **project and deflect** their own anger.
8. Even though I might be furiously angry, when I confront another person, in order to ensure that he/she truly hears my concerns, I must **speak in a normal and reasonable manner.**

9. The old saying "That was the straw that broke the camel's back" refers to someone having **reached their point of psychological overload from holding anger inside.**

10. My fourteen-year-old tells me that a nice quiet, meek, and timid boy in his class is being bullied by a few of the older students. I should **alert the school administrator to step in before a disaster occurs (and also advise my child to stay away from both the bullies and their target).**

Chapter Fourteen

Handling Extremely Aggressive Behavior and Potentially Violent Conflict

WHEN ANOTHER PERSON TAKES AN aggressive stance with you, they are either very angry about something and directing their anger at you, or they are trying to intimidate you into letting them have their way. In the first instance, they may, in fact, be angry with you about something you did or didn't do. The second instance is purely about manipulation.

Despite the fact that it requires a great deal of energy, out-of-control anger is sometimes utilized as a manipulative tactic for an individual to get his/her own way. We see this in young children who have temper tantrums.

Aggressive *verbal* behavior includes such things as loaded words; accusations; subjective, insulting terms; "you" statements that blame or label; and sarcastic, caustic, rude remarks. Aggressive *nonverbal* behavior includes such things as hands on hips, feet apart in a blocking posture; arms crossed across chest; a rigid or still posture; clenched fists; abrupt gestures; finger-pointing; fist pounding; or cold, staring, expressionless, and narrowed eyes. The tonal quality of the voice could be harsh, tense, shrill, strident, loud, or demanding, with a know-it-all or superior attitude.

For most of us, unfortunately, dealing with someone else's anger is enormously difficult. Some of us find the situation so disconcerting that, rather than attempting to deal with the other person's hostility, we will give in. We say yes when we'd rather say no, or tell the other person, "You're right; I was wrong," when we'd rather say, "I'm right; you're wrong." Using aggressive behavior becomes a very successful ploy in manipulation—because of that common reaction.

Another normal human reaction to someone else's aggressiveness is to become aggressive ourselves. Because we perceive another person's anger as directed at us, we feel attacked and in danger. In order to protect ourselves from that attack, we become angry ourselves. It is called *anger by contagion*. It makes no sense, but we do it anyway.

Therefore, when we are confronted by another person's anger, the first thing we should do is strengthen control over ourselves. We need to take deep breaths and will ourselves to relax. We must not get hooked into responding to the adversary's verbal onslaught.

Aggressive behavior toward another person is disrespectful. There is no valid excuse for verbally attacking someone. Aggressive behavior violates another person's psychological space. Therefore, what we need to do immediately, in a psychological sense, is put a line in the sand that says to the other person, "I will allow you to go only so far, but no further." To do that, we must stand up, so that we are level with our adversaries, hands at the side, and respond non-threateningly, but in a firm voice. We must not respond to the so-called charges but rather respond to the adversary's body language message. Then we should ask an open-ended question that begins with the words:

- What
- When
- Where
- Who
- How

Do not use *why* questions, because they are perceived as a criticism and will generally give you low-quality responses such as, "I don't know."

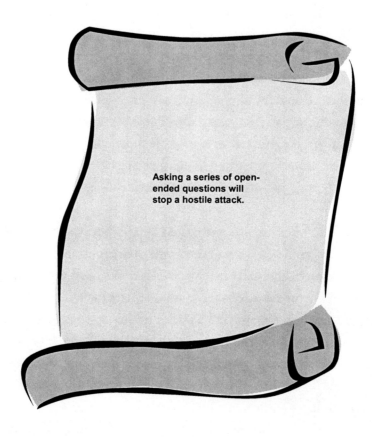

Asking a series of open-ended questions will stop a hostile attack.

For example, suppose a co-worker is livid about something you did, which made their work much harder. He or she confronts you aggressively, bellowing:

Livid: You know something? You're an absolute idiot. Do you realize that what you did makes it impossible for me to meet my deadline on my research project?

You:	I understand you're angry with me. I can hear it in your voice. What exactly did I do?
Livid:	You gave the research figures to MIS before I could get my hands on them. Now I have to wait until after they process them before I can utilize the data.
You:	I'm sorry that happened. What can I do now to remedy the situation?
Livid:	If the raw data is still on your computer, I can use that.
You:	Yes, it is still on my computer. Would you like to print it out yourself or would you prefer that I get it for you?
Livid:	You print it out. I'll just stand here and wait for it.
You:	Okay.

In this example, the attacked person asked a series of open-ended questions, which forced the angry person to think before answering. No explanation or excuses were given. Moreover, all questions were about remedying the situation.

There is an interesting physiological reason why asking a series of open-ended questions stops a hostile attack. Emotions are ruled by the right side of the brain. Thinking, language, and decision-making are ruled by the left side of the brain. By asking questions that require an angry person to think, you actually force them to switch from operating on the emotional side of their brain, where the anger and rage resides, to the side of the brain that contains language, thinking, and logic. Almost like magic, the anger behavior disappears.

Left Brain-Right Brain: How They Work

Left Brain   ## Right Brain

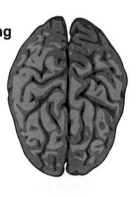

Rational, logical thinking   **Visualization**

Problem-solving   **Day dreaming**

Analysis of facts   **Experimental**

Organized; planned   **Gut Reaction**

Controlled   **Emotional**

Procedural;sequential   **Expressive**

Exhibit feelings

By starting your response with an acknowledgment of the other person's anger, you legitimize it and make it unnecessary for him/her to continue using it to make a point. Here is another example.

Irate:	I swear to God, if I hear "I just want to observe your work for another year" one more time, I will quit. You've had four years to observe. Either tell me I have no future here, or promote me! For once in your life, be straight with me!
Mgr:	I know you're frustrated over the lack of movement in your career. I can hear it in your voice. What do you think is holding you back?
Irate:	You.
Mgr:	What did we discuss about education during our last performance discussion?
Irate:	I need to finish my college degree. But Russell Raven never completed his degree, and he's now running a department.

Mgr:	How many years ago did that happen?
Irate:	Seven or eight.
Mgr:	How have our work, skill set, and educational requirements changed over that period of time?
Irate:	Everything's more technical; computer skills are a fundamental necessity. But I already have computer skills.
Mgr:	What about the educational requirements? How have they changed?
Irate:	No one gets hired into the organization without a college degree. But I should get grandfathered or something. After all, I've been here for four years. That's got to be worth something.
Mgr:	How did you make the decision that the rules should not apply to you?
Irate:	I didn't mean that, exactly. It's just that after eight grueling hours of work, it's tough to go to school for three hours. Besides, I've got a family. Don't they deserve to have me spend time with them?
Mgr:	I recognize how difficult it is to face such decisions. What do you think you should do?
Irate:	So all that's holding me back is the lack of a college degree? I'd be promoted if I had that degree?
Mgr:	You know I can't make those kinds of promises. A lot depends on the management vacancies available, as well as the continued good quality of your work. However, I can promise you that a college degree will get you on the list for promotional consideration. So, what will you do?
Irate:	I don't know. I really don't want to go to night school. That's a lot of pressure. Also, it doesn't guarantee that I'll get promoted. Isn't there some other way?

Mgr:	Not that I know of. What do you think your next step should be?
Irate:	Maybe if I took a few of those training courses Personnel offers. Couldn't you talk to Personnel and see about making an exception?
Mgr:	No. I think it would be better if you did that, so you could learn the answer for yourself. So, what will you do?
Irate:	I've got to think about this; maybe talk to my family. I'll get back to you.

All during your conversation with the angry person, it is critical to maintain direct eye contact and give them your full attention.

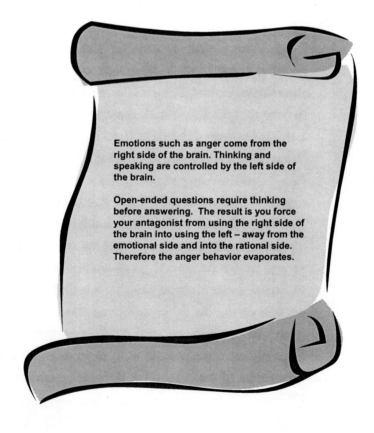

Emotions such as anger come from the right side of the brain. Thinking and speaking are controlled by the left side of the brain.

Open-ended questions require thinking before answering. The result is you force your antagonist from using the right side of the brain into using the left – away from the emotional side and into the rational side. Therefore the anger behavior evaporates.

Handling Potentially Violent Conflict (rage)

Recent studies released by the FBI profilers in Quantico, Virginia, have described those most likely to become violent in the work situation as male, white, between the ages of twenty-five and fifty-three, living alone, loners, maintaining a collection of guns or knives, and talking about weapons quite a bit.

The origin of the hostility comes from two sources:

- The person feels under attack and in great danger.
- The person is experiencing the frustration of unmet, maybe even unspoken, expectations.

A person's hostility may have nothing at all to do with you. You are just the nearest person in the room, so you get the brunt of the attack. Your best protection is your own visceral intelligence—in other words, listen to your gut. In addition, read the other person's body language and nonverbal messages, which will signal you that an attack is imminent. Be aware that psychic modifiers, such as alcohol or drugs, may be playing a part. Notice unsteady gait, slurred speech, and dilated pupils.

In most instances when violent conflict occurs in the workplace, it occurs in front of an audience. For some reason, your adversary requires spectators to witness their frenzied outburst. Rarely does this type of behavior happen one-on-one in private.

Once you see that trouble is coming, get yourself ready for the ordeal. First of all, slow down your physical movements and your mental traffic. Formulate a safety or escape plan. How close is the door? Is there a desk or barrier between you and the adversary? Can you dive under the desk if necessary? Tell yourself to be ready for anything. Finally, remember that you must respect the adversary's reality. Your goal in this situation must be to:

- Protect yourself from harm.
- Prevent the situation from escalating.
- Attempt to diffuse it.

The most important thing you can do is maintain a non-threatening body posture. Above all, do not look scared or intimidated, as that will encourage more hostility from your adversary. Do not back up or turn away from him or her. Stand up straight, arms at your sides, palms open. Speak in a calm, firm, and soothing tone. Avoid making physical contact. In fact, maintain a sizable physical distance between you and the adversary. If the area is crowded with people and furniture, suggest continuing the conversation in another, more spacious location. The adversary may be reacting to extreme pressure from some situation. He may feel cornered and see no conceivable way out of his problem. A more spacious location may relieve his sense of feeling trapped.

Give the adversary your full attention by maintaining strong, steady eye contact. Do not allow other people or sounds to distract you. Physically showing the adversary that you are paying 100 percent attention to what he is trying to communicate could save your life. It may be that the person feels that no one has ever listened to his concerns. Do not try to read the adversary's mind, and certainly do not try to interpret his motives. Do not argue or attempt to offer advice. *Just listen.* This is tricky, but you can attempt to diffuse the adversary's energy by distracting him. For example, you might say, "How about a cup of coffee?" or "Let's go get a smoke."

Whatever the adversary says, do not allow yourself to get hooked by his abusive language, manipulative questions, or statements made in the heat of battle. Answer reasonably. Forget about using logic. Anger is about feelings, so logic cannot possibly help here. Therefore, do not deny the person their rage or attempt to trivialize their feelings by saying such things as:

- "You shouldn't get so upset about that."
- "I understand how you feel."
- "Why don't you just take a deep breath and calm down."

It is critical that you think before you speak in these situations because you want to avoid escalating things. Take plenty of time before you say anything. Use *I messages* and words of support. For example, you might say:

- "No wonder you're upset. I'd be upset about that too."
- "Perhaps you're right."
- "I understand exactly what you're saying."

Look for an opportunity to exit the scene as soon as possible.

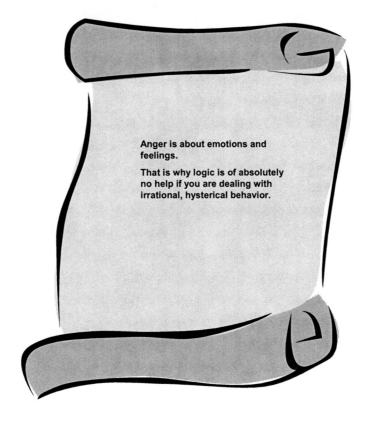

Anger is about emotions and feelings.

That is why logic is of absolutely no help if you are dealing with irrational, hysterical behavior.

All of the advice above is useless if you see that your adversary is armed. In such a situation, your only goal is to save yourself. Get out of the line of fire. Get out of the adversary's line of sight. Do not attempt to engage your adversary in any way. Try not to show fear by screaming or expressing terror through your body language. If you cannot see a way to quickly exit the scene unnoticed by the adversary, falling to the floor and lying very still might just save your life. Don't try to be a hero. Leave that to others who may be able to approach the adversary from behind. What you want to do is show the adversary physically that he/she faces no threat where you are concerned. Here is another true story.

Antwan was the first in his family to graduate from college. His family was so proud. They were unaware how much he had struggled and how much he hated college. After graduation, Antwan took a job with one of the nation's largest brokerages as a trainee. He was given a guaranteed salary of six hundred dollars per month for eight months, during which time he was being trained to develop his own stable of clients to whom he would be selling stocks, bonds, and mutual funds. At the end of that time period, Antwan's salary would be made up entirely of commissions from the products he sold to his clients.

Every day he left for work in a suit and tie, carrying a leather briefcase. His family was so proud. He was going into the city's financial center to a tall building of glass and granite. Antwan told his family his tiny cubical was a grand office, that he had a secretary, and that he was an important man in the company. His family was so proud.

This young trainee dutifully attended all the training classes and endured all the one-on-one coaching he received from his boss, Phil, the general manager. However, Antwan found that he hated cold-calling. In fact, he disliked every aspect of sales. At the end of eight months, his boss, Phil told Antwan that he had not made a successful transition from broker-trainee to broker and that he would be let go. The young man begged to be given another chance. He even shed a few tears and promised to work harder at becoming the broker he knew he could be. Phil told Antwan, as kindly as possible, that obviously sales were not his forte. He should therefore clean out his desk and leave. Antwan took the news very hard. Observers stated that the young man seemed to be in a trance, as he went to his cubicle to clean out his things. Several minutes later Antwan walked back to Phil's office and, from the doorway, shot him eight times, killing both him and his administrative assistant, Luann May. Several employees took Antwan down from behind in a football tackle. Antwan was still attempting to fire his gun, now empty of bullets, in the direction of his dead boss when his co-workers took him down.

Now let us look at an example that illustrates the effectiveness of showing a violent adversary physically that he/she faces no threat from you. The bank refused to help recently unemployed Peter with his mortgage. When Peter received his notice of foreclosure, he took a gun and stormed into the bank, taking sixteen people hostage, including the bank president. The police were dispatched to defuse the situation. The goal of the police swat team was to get everyone out of the bank without anyone being injured. Peter was wild and uncontrollable in his rage. By phone, the police negotiator, Fred, quietly begged Peter to allow him inside, so they could talk and find a way to resolve the problem. When Peter said he didn't trust Fred, the negotiator told Pete to go to the window where he would show Peter that he had nothing to fear from him. As Peter watched, Fred slowly stripped off his clothing, until he was only in his under-shorts.

That unexpected act immediately changed the dynamic of the situation. Peter allowed Fred to enter the bank. In a ten-minute conversation, the bank president promised the police and specifically their negotiator Fred as well as Peter that the bank would rescind the notice of foreclosure and arrange for a six-month moratorium on payments. During that six months, the bank would rewrite Peter's mortgage so that he would have a lower payment schedule.

Exercises for Chapter Fourteen

Directions: Shown below are some typical anger situations. Decide how best to handle each one, and place a checkmark beside your choice.

1. You are faced with another person's uncontrollable, hostile anger. It is extremely disconcerting and very frightening. Which one of the following reactions do you think might be your most effective strategy?
    *   Mentally run away by tuning the person out.
    *   Quickly agree to whatever the angry person says or wants.
    *   Offer the angry person some M&Ms or jelly beans.
    *   Say, "I can see that you are upset. What happened?"
    *   Get just as angry right back.
    *   Make some excuse that you to be somewhere else and leave.

2. A very effective method for dealing with an aggressive co-worker is to
    *   Stay away from him.
    *   Keep a weapon handy, and make sure your co-worker knows you are armed.
    *   No matter what he says, respond calmly with a question that cannot be answered by yes or no.

- Tell him you're happy to discuss anything with him as soon as he stops being so aggressive.
- Remind him that aggressive behavior encourages reprisal.

3. Those most likely to become violent in the work situation are male, white, between the ages of twenty-five and fifty-three, live alone, are loners, maintain a collection of guns or knives, and talk about weapons quite a bit.
   - True
   - False

4. Which of the following are the proven sources of violent hostility in a work setting?
   - The person is on psychic modifiers, such as alcohol or drugs.
   - The person believes he is under attack and/or in great danger.
   - The person is under extreme pressure from some situation; he/she feels cornered and sees no way out of the predicament.
   - The person is extremely angry and has no skills in anger management.
   - The person is reacting to the frustration of unmet, maybe even unspoken, expectations.
   - The person believes he/she has been taken advantage of one too many times.

5. You are dealing with a conflict situation, which you believe might quickly become violent. What should you do?
   - Ignore your gut feelings. Assume nothing violent is going to happen.
   - Forget about problem-solving; work on de-escalating and defusing the situation.
   - Make a threat in a loud, strong voice.
   - Say something distracting, such as, "Do you smell smoke?"
   - Suggest a ten-minute break.
   - Make a joke.
   - Run like hell.

6. You have a good friend who refuses to discuss issues about which she is in conflict. This person attempts to resolve her feelings of anger by engaging in annoying behaviors and common blunders, which can be easily explained away as actual mistakes. Her marriage relationship is suffering. She asks for your advice on what to do.
   - Ask her, "What are you so angry about?"
   - Explain that you are not qualified to give such advice.
   - Suggest she seek professional help.
   - Tell her to make up a list of the issues that are causing her anger, after which you will help her design a speech that will help clear everything up.
   - Offer to have a talk with her spouse on her behalf.
   - Advise her that if this sneaky, hostile behavior doesn't stop, she will quickly face a divorce.

Answers to Chapter Fourteen Exercises

1. You are faced with another person's loud-mouthed, hostile anger …

   In such a situation, the most effective method is to say, in an assertive voice, "I can see that you are upset. What happened?"

   The most common response in such a situation is probably to mentally run away by tuning the person out. The thought process here is, "It must be Agnes's time of the month," or "I guess George didn't get any last night." In other words, the person's anger is totally discounted.

   When a person makes a habit of such outbursts, their co-workers begin to look at him as emotionally unreliable and say things like, "You'd better look out for George. You never know what's going to set him off." Once that happens, career-wise, George will go nowhere.

2. A very effective method for dealing with an aggressive co-worker is …

   The answer here is, no matter what he or she says, respond calmly with a question that cannot be answered by yes or no. Anger is an emotion and is therefore ruled by the right side of the brain. Open-ended questions require a person to think before responding. Thinking is ruled by the left side of the brain. Therefore, when you ask an emotional person an open-ended question, you are forcing him or her to move from using one side of their brain to using the other in order to answer you. The result is that the person immediately stops being so emotional and begins to use a more rational approach.

3. Those most likely to become violent in the work situation are male, white …

    This is true. So, what's your defense? Engage your intuition. Listen to your hunches. Remember always that your gut is never wrong. Be aware of those around you. Notice extreme loner behavior and behavior that seems off-center. Take note of those who speak excessively about weapons and gun collections. Talk to management if you are concerned about a particular individual.

4. Proven sources of violent hostility in a work setting are …

    All the items mentioned would be considered contributing factors. However, two major sources of workplace violence are:
    - The person is reacting to the frustration of unmet, maybe even unspoken, expectations.
    - The person believes he is under attack and/or in great danger.

    For example, take the issue of being threatened with termination for wrongdoing. Loss of one's livelihood may mean not being able to pay for food, mortgage, car loan, etc. It would be easy for the person to believe he is in great danger. Let's add to that the fact that in his performance appraisal session six months ago, he was so lauded for some project he worked on that he believed he would be promoted soon. No one made any promises to him, but he had that expectation. Now, faced with the threat of termination, he is also reacting to a sense of frustration over unmet expectations. Now we have the perfect combination for a serious and violent (rage) explosion.

5. If you are dealing with a conflict situation that you believe may become violent ...

   You have two good choices here:

   - Forget about problem-solving; work on de-escalating and defusing the situation.
   - Suggest a ten-minute break.

   The point is, you need to change the environment, either psychology or physically, and you need to do it quickly.

6. You have a good friend who refuses to discuss issues ...

   You have two good alternatives here"

   - Explain that you are not qualified to give such advice
   - Suggest she seek professional help.

   Your friend is engaging in passive-aggressive behavior in a close and personal relationship. You do not want to put yourself in the middle of it. You have no way of knowing when (or if) a big hostile explosion will occur. You do not want one of the parties to accuse you of causing it with your meddling.

Chapter Fifteen

The Technique of Mediation

MEDIATION REFERS TO THE THIRD-PARTY intervention activity that creates, by communication alone, the climate, environment, and context that empowers people to generate their own solutions to the conflict issues existing between them.

For the most part, the mediator accomplishes this through verbal traffic management. In other words, the mediator's task is to keep the combatants' focus on problem-solving the issues rather than on one another's personality shortcomings, dumb decisions, and stupid behaviors.

It is essential that the mediator not take sides. Not only must the mediator be objective, it is crucial that he/she *not* have a personal stake in the composition and makeup of the final resolution. The only outcome that the mediator should favor is that the combatants resolve their differences.

If you manage others, it is quite possible that two of your staff members might ask for your assistance in helping them resolve a work conflict that is negatively impacting their productivity.

The first thing you would want to do is arrange for a private meeting time and place where there will be no distractions or interruptions. Once that is done, you need to tell both combatants, face to face and at the same time, how to prepare for the meeting. Tell them they need to create written documents with facts, data, dates, numbers, and other objective pieces of information that will support their individual view of the problem.

Once your assistance has been solicited, do *not* speak to one combatant unless the other is there to hear what is being said. This is necessary, so that you can maintain the trust of the combatants by ensuring them of your fairness and impartiality. If you speak to one without the other being present, you will create mistrust and suspicion regarding your objectiveness.

Setting Up the Mediation Room

The mediation room needs to have the following items:

- one five-by-three-foot table
- three chairs
- three easels with flip-chart paper
- one roll of masking tape
- several black, red, and green markers.

No refreshments are ever served in a mediation discussion. This is because:

- The presumption must be reinforced that this is *not* a social event.
- Refreshments encourage off-topic conversation (pass the sugar, any more buns left? etc.).
- Consuming the goodies brings in a different class of body language cues.

The combatants should be seated side by side and facing you across the table. You should sit with your back toward the front of the room and facing the combatants. Behind you, there should be an easel with a flip chart for your use.

Seating the combatants side by side makes it more difficult for them to make negative gestures and facial comments at one another as each listens to the other speaking. Allowing the combatants to sit across from one another will only strengthen their adversarial stance toward one another. Seating the parties beside one another gives you a better chance for movement toward resolution.

Place each one of the two remaining easels with flip-chart paper opposite the combatants, so that each has one directly in front of him or her at the front of the room. You will be using one flip chart for each combatant. The process calls for you to note down the points each combatant makes on his or her individual flip chart. As each page is filled up, you will tear it off and paste it on the side wall closest to that combatant.

Utilizing flip charts in this manner makes it unnecessary for the combatants to keep restating their individual view of things. In conflict management, it is always helpful to surround people with their data. Seeing things in writing allows people to find places where negotiation is possible. It also reinforces those areas in which the combatants agree. Best of all, this strategy unfailingly makes the mediation process move along very quickly.

Diagram of Mediation Room Setup

Beginning the Mediation Session

Open the meeting by asking each combatant individually, "Do you want to solve this problem?" This may sound like a needless step to you, but, in order for you to succeed at the task of mediation, you need the solid commitment of both combatants to the exercise of problem-solving.

Once you have their commitment to work on problem-solving, it is time for you to make your expectations clear. This is when you tell the combatants that your purpose is to assist them to generate a resolution that they both can live with and that will solve the conflict. You are *not* going to solve their problem for them; they are going to do that.

You also want to make it clear that you will remain impartial and objective throughout. You will be asking questions when clarification is needed. You will also redirect the conversation to ensure that the interaction remains on track. Tell the combatants that you do *not* have a stake in the shape of the outcome. Your only goal is that, at the end of the meeting, there is an agreed-upon resolution. Moreover, you will *not* judge whether the agreed outcome is fair. As long as both parties consent to it, you will have done your job.

The next thing you want to do is lay down the ground rules. You might say something like this:

"First of all, it is important that we all agree anything said in this room is confidential. We must respect the privacy of one another's opinions, feelings, and information.

"Secondly, while one of you is speaking, the other must remain quiet and listen. I am the only person in this room who's allowed to interrupt, and when I do, it will be for matters of clarification only.

"Thirdly, you two must refrain from making disparaging statements or displaying negative body language toward each other. It does not help the problem-solving process.

"Fourthly, I expect both of you to be honest, objective, specific, and straightforward in your speaking. For my part, if I read questionable messages in your body language, I will immediately ask that you say what's on your mind.

"Finally, we will not dwell on past mistakes or problems. We will focus on the issue at hand without rehashing old data."

Your next step would be to ask one combatant to present his or her side of the problem. While the first combatant is speaking, you capture the salient points on the flip chart assigned to that combatant. Utilize the combatant's own words as much as possible. When a flip-chart sheet is filled up with notes, rip it off the pad and, using the masking tape, stick those notes on the wall at the side where that combatant is seated.

Part of your job here is to make certain the reporting combatant is not interrupted by the other combatant. After the first combatant has spoken, you should ask the second combatant to describe his or her understanding of what he or she just heard. Again, make sure the second combatant is not interrupted. When the second combatant has finished his or her statement of the other's position, you should ask the first combatant if the other got it right. If the answer is no, ask the first combatant to clarify his or her position again. Keep going back and forth in this manner until the first combatant is certain the second combatant has a solid understanding of the position. Then you have to repeat this strategy with the second combatant. During this time, you will be noting all important points on the appropriate flip chart.

While each combatant is explaining his or her side of the problem, you can help clarify what is being said by saying such things as:

- "Can you try harder to explain what you mean?"
- "Can you say that in another way?"
- "What does this have to do with the issue at hand?"
- "Try to be specific; utilize facts and data, not personalities."
- "Please restate that without the personal disparagement."
- "That sounded disrespectful."
- "Please make your point using objective, not subjective, data."

- "Here is what I heard you say _____"
- "In other words, you would like to _____."
- "It sounds to me as if you're saying _____."
- "Let me be sure I've got this right _____."
- "What did you mean by _____?"

If the combatant's conversation strays from the problem at hand, in order to refocus the discussion, you might say such things as:

- "Please refocus on the topic at hand."
- "How can we get back on track?"

Surrounding people with their data:
    prevents the repetition of issues
    speeds the negotiation process
    keeps everyone on track
    makes it easier to see where
    agreement is possible

The idea is to make certain that each combatant thoroughly understands the other person's view of the problem. Once that is accomplished, you can take your seat at the table, facing the combatants. Ask the combatants to look at the data now displayed on the walls, and ask if either of them sees a way their problem might be solved. Encourage the combatants to make changes to their own data on the flip-chart papers. Perhaps one will say, "Let's forget about this item; I can handle it another way." Maybe one will say, "I'd like us to negotiate on this item."

In conflict, combatants tend to lump issues together that only further inflame the other party. This is known as the *kitchen sink syndrome*. The problem begins to sound like a mass of indistinguishable complaints. As long as many issues are intertwined, it will be almost impossible for the combatants to negotiate, fix, or resolve their situation.

If you, as the mediator, can help the combatants to create separations between the elements in the conflict, it can produce a significant shift in the combatants' ability to approach the resolution process more constructively. Here is what you are trying to help the combatants do:

- Separate positions from interests.
- Separate people from problems.
- Separate problems from solutions.
- Separate symptoms from causes.
- Separate complaints and gripes from problems and difficulties.
- Separate areas of agreement from areas of disagreement.
- Separate the future from the past and the past from the present.
- Separate emotion from logic.
- Separate facts from assumptions.
- Separate process from content.

- Separate options and choices from wishes and whims.
- Separate communicated expectations from unspoken expectations.
- Separate criteria from selection.
- Separate one combatant's needs from the other's needs.

At this point in the mediation process, you should ask the following questions to assist the combatants in moving forward in their problem-solving effort:

- "What other way might there be for you to attack this problem?"
- "What have you identified as the real, underlying, foundational cause of the problem?"
- "What other alternatives might there be?"
- "What other information might help you solve this problem?"
- "What else might be important to consider?"

Remember that your mission is to push the combatants toward exposing the root of their conflict, forcing them to stay on point, and, finally, helping them negotiate an outcome with which they both can live.

It is important to jump in immediately whenever you observe unhelpful body language. The strategy is to compel the combatant to speak the truth of what their body language is insinuating. Here are some helpful comments for doing that:

- "Your body language tells me you disagree with his [or her] statement."
- "My sense is that you are not happy with that as a solution."
- "I can tell there's more to the story than what you've just related."
- "Don't roll your eyes; tell him [or her] what you think."

- "That doesn't sound very convincing."
- "You sound unsure and hesitant."

Always keep in mind that they have to find their own solution. You can't do it for them. And, the more of themselves they put into the solution-finding effort, the more likely the solution they choose will work.

As the discussion continues, your critical task is to ensure that the combatants do not interrupt one another. As the combatants begin to propose possible solutions to their conflict, you can note those choices on the flip chart assigned to you. This time, however, when you post these sheets on the wall, paste them at the front of the room, directly opposite the combatants, so they can easily see them as they continue their deliberations.

Securing the Outcome

When the combatants finally come to a decision, give each of them a piece of paper and ask that they write out his or her decision and sign it. Check to make certain that both parties have written down the identical decision or solution.

Now you have to move into the final phase of the mediation process, which is the development of an action plan to implement the decision. Ask the combatants how they plan to implement their decision. Once again, utilize your flip chart at the front of the room to capture their ideas. Question them, if necessary, to ensure clarity. Insist that they designate who will do what, and make sure that each action has a date on which that activity will be accomplished. During this phase, you might want to use some of the following comments:

- "What would need to be done first?"
- "Who specifically should do this?"
- "How do you know these dates are realistic?"
- "What obstacles might you encounter?"

- "What resources would you need that you do not already have?"
- "Who might be willing to help you?"
- "How will you know your solution has been successful?"
- "How will you ensure that the same problem does not reoccur in the future?"

Ask each combatant to make a copy of the action plan. You, too, should make a copy of both the decision and the action plan for your notes. Ninety days after your mediation discussion, you might want to send the combatants a copy of these two documents through interoffice mail, with a cover note that says, "How's it going?" That lets the combatants know that you expect they followed through and did the work necessary to permanently resolve their conflict. Here is a sample of a Memo of Understanding that can be utilized to conclude and secure the results of a formal mediation process.

MEMO OF UNDERSTANDING BETWEEN
James Bond and Rambo Smith

Date of the agreement

1. This memo represents the complete understanding between the parties regarding the terms and conditions of their agreement.

2. Whatever is contained in this memo supersedes any oral statements that might have been made regarding a mutual solution to the problem.

3. A list of the terms of the agreement including statements about who is to do what by which specific date.

4. Main tasks/responsibilities of each combatant

    Standards for each task

    Date of completion of each task

    Any confidentiality restrictions

5. A list of the benefits that accrue to each combatant with the resolution of their problem.

6. A place for you and the combatants to sign and date, signifying the acceptance and agreement of all parties to the terms of their resolution.

_____   _____   _____
Date   Combatant #1   Combatant #2   Mediator

The Role of the Mediator

Now that you understand how to prepare for and carry out a mediation session, let's examine your role in the mediation process more closely.

Perhaps one of the most interesting characteristics of the mediator role is that you don't have to fully understand the problem in order to be effective in your role. In fact, your preparation is all about getting the space ready where the discussion will take place. It does not include any investigation of the facts. That is because conflict requiring third-party intervention is often about emotions. Objective facts gathered by an outsider rarely help the conflicted parties. The fact gathering is something they must do, because they have to own the entire process.

Among the skills required for mediation or facilitation is the ability to remain open-minded, attentive, and accepting in the sense of being nonjudgmental, interested, and encouraging. Because body language is a key in getting to the bottom of things, you have to be proficient at *listening visually*. This means you must be able to recognize the meaning beyond the words. More often than not, the true meaning is conveyed by the body language and tone of voice, while the manufactured, and perhaps less than honest, response is carried by the words.

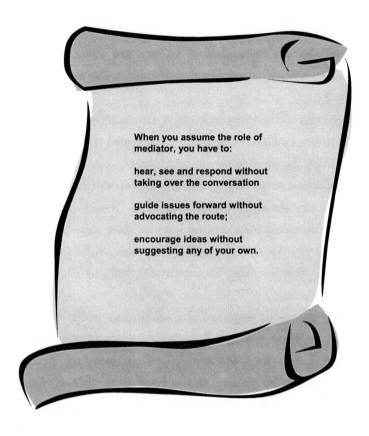

When you assume the role of mediator, you have to:

hear, see and respond without taking over the conversation

guide issues forward without advocating the route;

encourage ideas without suggesting any of your own.

As the mediator, you have to monitor your own body language carefully. You are requiring that the combatants be honest and direct in their communications. You, therefore, need to model those qualities yourself. In other words, don't make faces, roll your eyes, or sigh at anything the combatants say. Make no derogatory remarks about the behavior of the combatants. None of that helps the resolution process.

You should consider yourself personally responsible for achieving an outcome that leaves the combatants concurring on a course of action. Again, your responsibility does not extend to judging the fairness of the outcome, only to obtaining an outcome to which both combatants agree. It is important that you achieve a balance between being supportive and caring and being assertively direct and meticulously clear about their roles and your expectation that they find their own solution.

It takes two to tangle. Both combatants, therefore, must share the responsibility for the conflict or problem. Both must also share the responsibility for finding a resolution with which both can live. You are merely assisting the combatants to clarify their communication to each other. Your mission is to ensure that both combatants not only understand the words but also the meaning behind the words.

In the latter stages of your mediation discussion, you will be assisting the combatants to assume responsibility for their resolution activities and the accountability for the results of those activities.

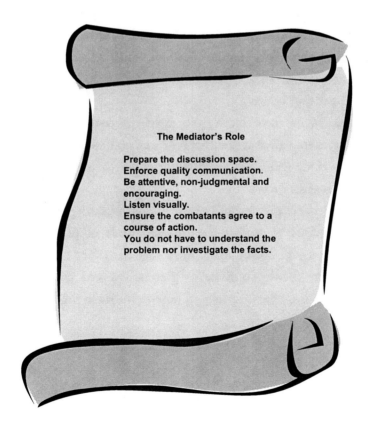

The Mediator's Role

Prepare the discussion space.
Enforce quality communication.
Be attentive, non-judgmental and encouraging.
Listen visually.
Ensure the combatants agree to a course of action.
You do not have to understand the problem nor investigate the facts.

Think of yourself as the enforcer of quality communication. First of all, insist on concrete, substantive statements. Make sure that whatever a combatant says is specific and easily understood by both you and the other combatant. Secondly, ensure that all communication by the combatants is respectful communication. Whatever is expressed should not target the weaknesses of the other or the stupidity of their mistakes. You want the combatants to focus on issues, goals, data, and difficulties that need to be resolved.

As verbal traffic director, you ensure that each combatant is successful at fully explaining his or her position and ideas. Mostly, however, you keep quiet, observe, and listen. You only break into the conversation for purposes of clarification. When you do interject, it is done with a question that cannot be answered by yes or no. You help clarify the combatants' thinking by capturing their issues on flip-chart paper. This also assists the combatants to define the limits of their problem. If the combatants go off track, you ask questions which refocus and clarify the purpose of your meeting. When pointing out negative body language, you are frank and honest.

At the end of the exercise, you assist the combatants to create a tangible, written plan of action that both can point to as their resolution. You keep written records of assignments and decisions, so that you can follow up in ninety days.

You may not realize it, but in your role as mediator you are teaching your combatants to utilize the rational tools of problem-solving. Hopefully you will be the inspiration that motivates the combatants to handle any future conflicts by themselves and without outside intervention. Now they understand how to work the process.

The Goal of the Mediation

- To generate a solution with which both parties can live
- The solution must resolve their problem
- Whether the outcome is fair, balanced or equal is not important
  – only that the parties have agreed to it

Chapter Fifteen Exercises

Directions: Respond to the following issues by placing a checkmark beside the response you believe will best serve the situation. As always, the correct responses and explanations follow.

1. You have been asked by two of your staff members to mediate a conflict they are having with one another. This means what you should do is:
   - Solve the problem for them.
   - Listen to both sides, and then decide who's right and who's wrong.
   - Investigate the facts, and tell them what you learned.
   - Make it possible for both of them to find their own solution.
   - Study the issue, collect the facts, and explore all sides of the problem.
   - Judge the fairness of their solution when they come up with something.

2. As a mediator in a conflict, your most important job is to:
   - Set up the discussion room.
   - Ask Personnel to handle it.
   - Arrange for coffee and donuts.
   - Listen carefully to the discussion.

- Observe and comment on the body language of the combatants.
- Operate as a verbal traffic director.
- Provide feedback to the combatants.

3. Among the skills required for effective mediation or facilitation are:
    - the ability to analyze problems
    - the ability to look interested even when you're not
    - the ability to read body language
    - the ability to shoot a handgun with remarkable accuracy
    - the ability to be nonjudgmental, even in the face of really dumb ideas
    - the ability to jump on a good resolution idea when you hear it

4. Two of your employees are involved in a bitter personal conflict. It is beginning to affect the rest of the staff negatively. Your best strategy for dealing with this is:
    - Intervene and offer to mediate a settlement to their dispute.
    - Get the two of them together; tell them their quarrel is affecting the rest of the staff and that you want it stopped immediately.
    - Fire one of the parties.
    - Get the two of them together and tell them to settle their differences immediately or they might find themselves looking for another job.
    - Meet with each person separately; hear both sides of the dispute; then you impose a settlement.
    - Since the conflict is personal, ignore it.

5. Studies show that in communication, the true meaning is conveyed by the body language and tone of voice, while the fabricated response is carried by the words. Assuming this is true, in a conflict situation where you are one of the combatants, you should:

- Ignore everything your opponent says.
- Study the meaning of body language cues before going into mediation.
- Carefully scrutinize the tone of voice, pace of words, and hesitations in speech of your opponent.
- Insist that your opponent be put in a straight jacket before conversation begins.
- If you think you see or hear a hidden message lurking behind the actual words of your opponent's body language, immediately ask for clarification.
- Studiously monitor your own body language to ensure you give nothing away.

6. You are attempting a mediation between your two boys, who have been fighting over who gets to use your car on prom night next weekend. Things have been moving along pretty well, when one of your sons says, "He just wants to use the car as a bedroom. He's so hot for Nancy, he can't wait to get her alone so he can do her." Your best strategy for dealing with this is:

- Tell your sons that neither of them can have the car.
- Suggest your son make sure he has plenty of condoms.
- Ask your other son, "Is that how you intend to use my car, as a cheap motel room?"
- Say, "I'm confused. What does this have to do with the issue at hand?"
- Explain to both boys that you do not want your car used in that way.

Answers to the Exercises of Chapter Fifteen

1. You have been asked by two of your staff members to mediate a conflict ...

    The correct response is: make it possible for both of them to find their own solution.

    If you have been asked to mediate a conflict resolution discussion, it probably means the two people involved are so embroiled in their situation that neither of them can gain enough of a perspective to see how things might be resolved. What they need is someone who can help each of them to hear the other person's view of the problem. They have to find their own solution, because they will have to live with it, and the more of their own efforts they put into the solution-finding process, the more likely that the solution they select will work. Like a referee in a boxing match, all they need you to do is separate them when they get into a clinch.

2. As a mediator in a conflict, your most important job is to ...

    The correct answer is operate as a verbal traffic director.

    The next-most-important task for the moderator is to set up the discussion room appropriately. The third-most-important item is to observe and comment on the body language of the combatants. The remaining items are unnecessary, especially the donuts, which will only distract from the real purpose of the meeting.

3. Among the skills required for effective mediation or facilitation are ...

    The answer here is the ability to read body language. You also need the ability to listen and to ask tactical questions that keep the combatants focused on resolving their conflict. You do not need any of the other items listed.

4. Two of your employees are involved in a bitter, personal conflict …

Since the conflict is personal, ideally you would like to ignore it and let them resolve the problem on their own. However, because their problem is affecting the staff negatively, you *must* step in. Your best choice of action here is to get the two of them together and tell them their quarrel is affecting the rest of the staff and that you want it stopped immediately. If they have any maturity at all, they will take care of the problem themselves. If they lack maturity, you may have to take a mediation stance with them.

5. Studies show that in communication, the true meaning is conveyed …

The correct response here is both the body language and tone of voice of your opponent; you should immediately ask for clarification if you think you see or hear a hidden message lurking behind the actual words. A simple statement, such as, "I sense that what I just said has made you a little angry," can really clear up problems before they start.

6. You are attempting to do a mediation between your two boys. The mediation strategy works exceedingly well in family situations. Children can constructively take part at a very early age and come out of a mediation feeling good at the result and stronger as a person. In this case, your stress level is being challenged, and you must not take the bait. You really don't know what your son's intentions are. This is a distraction. The best answer here is for you to say, "I'm confused. What does this have to do with the issue at hand?"

Chapter Sixteen

Managing Team Conflicts

THE NATURE OF WORK IN today's world forces many people to work in partnership rather than alone. Work groups or teams are the result of our technological sophistication and the recognition that it is no longer possible for one or two individuals to supply all the expertise that a particular project might require.

Management, therefore, brings together a collection of talented individuals and unites them behind a series of related goals. Management ensures that the achievement of these goals is something which the team members will find challenging, interesting, and career-enhancing. In addition, management makes a conscious effort to give the team the responsibility for decision-making regarding the work. The underlying assumption is that, given these things, these capable individuals will function effectively in a team setting, if they just remember to treat one another with respect, openness, trust, and sensitivity for individual differences.

This wonderful plan, however, does not deal with the reality of competition, conflict, and the struggle for power that are part of every job. The nature of teamwork means that the individuals involved are extremely dependent on one another for the achievement of the team's goals. Yet team members may spend a great deal of time playing win-lose games, working on hidden agendas, and, in effect, being competitive instead of being collaborative. As a result, the team's effectiveness suffers, and its goals are not achieved. In a team where win-lose drives and hidden agenda are prevalent, it is not safe for a person to be open. Team members may therefore experience little or no job satisfaction.

ICEBERG of TEAM CONFLICT

What management believes will solve the problem:

New systems & procedures

Different or more people

Revised policies

Larger budget

What is actually at the heart of the team's problems:

Is there an "in group" and am I a member of it?

Is there a team member with more power than I?

Is there team member who is trying to control me?

Are my skills being utilized appropriately?

Am I given the resources necessary to do my job properly?

Is it safe for me to confront my teammates with negative

feedback without fear of reprisal?

When teams are having difficulty fulfilling their missions, management steps in and may rearrange the systems, policies, and procedures under which the team is working, in an effort to help the team regain its capability. When that fails, management may change the mix of individuals on the team and provide the group with additional resources. What's interesting is this doesn't work either. What's destroying the team's ability to function effectively is well below the surface and involves individual team members who may be harboring all kinds of unspoken negative feelings, concerns relating to power and control, and hidden agendas of their own. What is going on below the surface is affecting the entire team in a negative way.

It is at this point that the manager or team leader calls for a *team-building* to uncover the problems and resolve them. As you can imagine, this is already pretty late in the game. Team members have become well entrenched in their negative behaviors. It is better if you can explain to your team early on that these negative drives are fairly normal within teams. Then give your team the tools for exposing and resolving such issues without outside intervention.

No matter how many individuals make up the team, if one person is harboring any of the following negative attitudes or concerns, the team will be rendered ineffective.

In-Out: Within the team, there may exist a tight-knit *in group*. These individuals might be favorites of the boss or gain the ear of the boss more readily than other team members. Whatever the case, there is another team member who feels left out, slighted, and marginalized. Their goals are not, therefore, focused on the team's mission, but rather on his or her own animosity at being rejected by the *in* group.

Power and Control: Each individual team member has the power to hinder and frustrate the work activities of all the other team members by simply not doing his or her share of the work or doing his or her portion poorly. Another team member is forced into taking up the slack and may feel bitter about being forced to do so. One team member may suspect that another team member is purposefully making her look incompetent by providing her with incorrect or incomplete information or training. The result is that the team member harbors a great deal of antagonism regarding the situation.

Skills and Resources: Sometimes an individual team member may believe that, although his skill set is being utilized appropriately in terms of the team's mission, management is not providing him with the resources to do the job. The result is the team member appears to be inept for the assignment. On the other hand, the team member may believe that his team task does not make use of his skill set, but rather confronts him where he is weak. The outcome is that he appears to be incapable of doing the job. The result, once again, is that the team member harbors a great deal of antagonism regarding his situation.

Openness, Confrontation, and Feedback: If a team is to function effectively, there must be openness, confrontation, and trust among individual team members. For example, if one team member is concerned about the way another team member is going about their individual assignment, it must be entirely appropriate and legitimate to confront that team member without fear of retaliation or reprisal. If things are not working as they should and timetables are slipping, the environment created by the team and its management must be a safe place in which to discuss problems and face the team member(s) involved, without fear of retribution.

To avoid letting these negative feelings undermine the team's effectiveness, you need to give your team the tools for exposing and resolving such issues. If you teach them how to do this without outside intervention, you strengthen the cohesiveness and power of the team. There are four methods you can use for assisting your team to resolve its own internal conflicts whenever they occur.

DeAnne Rosenberg

Engineering Consensus

The first conflict-solving strategy is known as *Engineering Consensus.* Let's say your team is in conflict about which among several alternatives they should take to achieve a particular goal. Your first step is to write the question or decision to be discussed on a flip chart. Then invite ideas and opinions from each member of the team, one at a time. Make sure each person has an equal chance to present his or her ideas.

Record exactly what each person says on the flip chart. Then have each team member take one minute to explain his or her idea or opinion in more detail to the group. Your next step is to solicit questions from the group. Allow about thirty seconds for this Q and A. Repeat this with each team member who provided data for the flip chart.

After every team member has had an opportunity to explain his or her stance on the issue, you should ask if team members wish to combine ideas, change their opinions, or withdraw their perspective altogether. Once those changes have been made, it is time to take a *weighted vote.*

A weighted voted is executed as follows. Each team member selects what he or she feels are the three best choices on the list of alternatives, and prioritizes their choices, by giving three points to their most favored item, two points for their next-favored item; and one point for their least-favored item. You record each member's ratings next to the ideas listed on the flip chart. Then you add up the numerical ratings for each item. The item with the highest number represents the group's consensus.

The Team as Facilitator Method

The second method is called *The Team as Facilitator Method.* Suppose the conflict is just between two of the members of your team. Their problem, however, is having a negative impact on the other team members. What you do is enlist the other, uninvolved, neutral team members to function as a group of mediators or facilitators to the combatants. Here is how this strategy works.

First you invite each of the combatants to state his or her view of the problem to the team. Insist there be no long speeches. Then ask the neutral team members to state what they think are the areas of agreement and the areas of disagreement. Post these separately on flip charts, one flip chart to record the points of agreement and a second flip chart to record the areas of disagreement.

Now ask the neutral team members to explore the areas of disagreement for specific issues. Encourage them to uncover and assert what they think are the basic or underlying problems. Record these on a third flip chart, and post this sheet at the front of the room.

Next, ask the combatants if either of them would care to suggest modifications to his or her stance on the issues. Resolution should be achieved at this point. In the event that no resolution has occurred, ask the team to step in and suggest methods by which the combatants' conflict might be resolved. List these suggestions on that third flip chart. Post this sheet at the front of the room. Now ask the combatants to accept one of the team's recommendations. When a choice has been made, you should formally summarize the solution to the group. Ask the team to assist the combatants in making the selected solution operational. You should then record the decision in writing and present each combatant with a copy.

Role Negotiation Method

A third method for resolving internal team conflicts is called *The Role Negotiation Method*. Of all the methods, this one is the most confrontational. It is recommended that this strategy be used only as a last resort—the one you would use before disbanding and reconstituting the team.

Let's say that you are a new manager or team leader, and you perceive that your group, overall, is not working as effectively as it should. In fact, there is so much tension that productivity is virtually at a standstill. You suspect that there is some low level of unspoken, unaddressed conflict going on, which has been the state of affairs for a long time. You want to raise the issues and get them resolved immediately.

At a team meeting, you distribute a stack of plain 4x6 inch white index cards to each team member, yourself included. Instruct each team member to complete three cards on each member of the team. This includes you, too.

One card is to say, "What I want Mary or Mark to keep doing, because, when they do these things, it makes my job easier."

One card is to say, "What I want Mary or Mark to stop doing, because, when they do these things, it makes my job more difficult."

The third card says, "What I think is the best quality Mary or Mark brings to the team."

The strategy is two cards which specify positive things and only one card that targets negative things. Moreover, those negative items are work related, not personality related.

The next step is to redistribute the cards so that each team member gets the cards which were written about him or her. Allow sufficient time for all team members to read their cards. Then ask that each team member decide which issues they are willing to discuss with the team and perhaps negotiate about changing their actions.

Supply each team member with a flip chart on which they can write those negotiable issues. As manager or team leader, you have to do this too—and you have to do it first. You do this in order to model the strategy for the team and to show them your willingness to change. You also want to model the open and frank discussion you wish your team members to have with their co-workers.

Now you want to initiate group discussion. The purpose of the discussion is to forge agreements whereby one team member agrees to do *X* if some other team member will agree to stop doing *Y*. By the way, as you might expect, no matter what lame issues a particular team member might put on his or her chart, once the discussion begins, that team member's real issues will be immediately exposed by the others on the team.

All agreements are put in writing. At the end of your session, you should ask each team member for a commitment to help all the others in keeping those agreements.

Conflict Analysis by the Team

The fourth and last method is called *Conflict Analysis by the Team*. With this method, you will play the role of the mediator to the entire team, and you will use a very structured format.

Let's say that your entire team is involved in the same conflict situation. It may be caused by another department whose information your team desperately needs to do its work. That department has been most uncooperative. It may be because one person on your team has become the source of divisiveness. It may be caused by something you did or did not do, such as obtaining a new software package that the team requested and you promised to get them.

Before the team meets for the conflict discussion, you will write out the following list of questions on flip chart paper, one sheet for each question. Mount all the sheets on the walls all around the meeting room. In this way, when the team responds to the questions, you can write down the comments and surround the team members with their data.

You will be asking each team member, one at a time, to respond to each of the questions. You will record the responses on the appropriate flip chart sheet for all to see. The questions are listed below.

- Who does this conflict affect?
- How does it affect him/her?
- What outcomes do you want to see from resolving the conflict?
- What has prevented this conflict from being discussed openly before?
- Describe the conflict situation briefly and objectively.
- Is there a pattern of conflict around this directive, department, or individual?
- What specific course of action will resolve the conflict?

After all team members have spoken, and you have captured their data on the flip chart paper, ask the team to examine the data on the walls. See if anyone wishes to change his or her responses. Allow him or her to do that. Now tell the team they have to determine what they think should be the next step.

At this point, you step into a mediator role and manage the verbal traffic, so that everyone is heard. Encourage the team to come to a consensus. Record the team's decision and action plan on the flip chart at the front of the room. After the meeting, you should send a hard copy of the team's decision and action plan to each team member.

With all these methods, action begins on items relating to the work. However, if the real issue is something in the realm of interpersonal relations, never fear. Once the discussion begins, the core issues will unfailingly jump to the forefront right away.

Methods for Resolving Internal Team Conflicts

Engineering Consensus	**ideal for sorting through alternatives**
Team as Facilitator	**when two of the team members are involved**
Role Negotiation	**when entire team is dysfunctional**
Conflict Analysis by the Team	**when the problem effects the entire team**

Exercises for Chapter Sixteen

Directions: Select the answer most likely to be successful in the following situations and place a checkmark beside your choice.

1. You are the team leader of six individuals drawn from different departments of the organization. The team's project, when completed, will be utilized by all areas of the company. Things are not going well. The team seems to be unable to get anything done. Deadlines are slipping, and team members seem uninvolved or disinterested. Your best strategy is:
    - Bring in a trainer who will initiate some team-building exercises.
    - Give the team a motivating speech about cooperation and teamwork.
    - Tell the team that they were brought together to solve a problem that is negatively affecting the entire organization. Their efforts are critical, and everyone is expecting great results from their efforts.
    - Since individual team members are probably busy with their own work, try holding your team meetings via telephone conferencing.
    - Provide each team member with written instructions as to what you want done, how he/she is to do it, and the date by which it is to be completed.

- State the problems; ask that the team members contribute their ideas for resolving the problems; you moderate the discussion.

2. You and your team are attempting to resolve a serious work problem between two of your team members. It immediately becomes obvious to you that one of the conflicted team members isn't really listening to what his/her co-workers have to say. Your most effective action here is:
   - Ask, "What are you thinking about right now?"
   - In a loud voice say, "Everyone here is trying to help you solve a problem. The least you can do is pay attention."
   - Ignore his/her body language.
   - Ask if he/she needs to go to the bathroom.
   - Ask, "Hello, are you with us?"
   - Say, "Your body language tells me you don't care whether or not this issue is resolved."

3. Your team members are in conflict over how various aspects of the project should be done and how the work should be split up among them. In order to sort things out once and for all, you will:
   - Take the team out for coffee and donuts.
   - Hold a vote where the majority wins.
   - Hold a meeting where you tell each member exactly what to do and how to do it.
   - Tell the team to roll up their sleeves and get these issues sorted out. Then you leave.
   - Talk to your manager to gain some perspective and maybe some good ideas for handling the problem.
   - Initiate the team process of engineering consensus to get things squared away.

4. You are a new employee. You are assigned to a team whose members have been working together for a long time. Right away you sense that these people have a good deal of deep-seated hostility toward one another. Your best course of action is:
    *   Suggest to the team leader that a serious *teambuilding* exercise is needed.
    *   Ask to be reassigned to another team.
    *   Start looking for another job.
    *   Determine which team member is the strongest, most influential individual, and try to become his/her protégée
    *   Go to Personnel/Human Resources, explain the situation, and ask them to advise you on what to do.
    *   It just might be that your observations are incorrect. Do nothing for a few months and see what happens.

5. One of your team members is not doing his fair share of the work. The rest of the team is being forced to pitch in to take up the slack. Everyone is complaining; motivation is at an all-time low; the team leader seems unaware that anything is amiss. Your best course of action is:
    *   Speak to your team leader and ask him/her to do something about the situation.
    *   Make sure that when the leftover work from the slacker comes around, you are too busy to take care of any of it.
    *   Take the slacker out for coffee and enlighten him as to the psychological damage he is inflicting upon the rest of the team.
    *   Get the team members together, and all of you make a formal complaint to the team leader's boss.

6. Your team has just gone through the process of *engineering consensus*. The team wholeheartedly voted against taking the course of action you believed was the most likely to achieve the best results. Your best course of action is:

    - Suck it up. The team voted against you. Now you must work as hard as you can to see that the team is as successful as possible.
    - Plan to sabotage the team's efforts. Show them you were right and they were wrong.
    - Demand a revote.
    - Since this was their plan, let them work it without you.

Answers to Chapter Sixteen Exercises

1. You are the team leader of six individuals drawn from different …

    Your best strategy here is to state the problems and then ask that the team members contribute their ideas for resolving the problems. The best tool for this is the *team as facilitator* strategy, while you moderate the discussion. The team probably cannot resolve these structural issues unaided. Members need someone to moderate their discussion, capture their concerns, and hear what each member has to say, before they can make any decisions.

2. You and your team are attempting to help resolve a serious work problem …

    Your most effective action here is to ask that team member what he/she is thinking about. You need to get them into the conversation without making any assumptions.

3. Your team members are in conflict over how various aspects …

    The choice that stands the best chance of getting everyone involved and committed to the project is to utilize the strategy of *engineering consensus*. In this way, team members make the decisions about who does what and in what order.

4. You are a new employee … Your best choice here is to start looking for another job. As a new employee, you have no credibility built up to make a *teambuilding* suggestion to your team leader or to ask

Personnel for a different assignment. While you wait for that new job, the alternative of *wait and see* might work for you.

5. One of your team members is not doing his or her fair share …

    This is why openness and trust among team members is so important—because the solution that will best solve this problem is to take the slacker out for coffee and enlighten him as to the psychological damage he is inflicting upon the rest of the team. If that strategy doesn't work, you should speak to the team leader.

6. The team voted against your recommendation …

    Your best answer here is: suck it up. The team voted against you. Now you must work as hard as you can to see that the team is as successful as possible. The purpose of engineering consensus is to ensure that the team speaks with one united voice and works toward its goals in a cohesive manner, with everyone on the same page.

Chapter Seventeen

Final Thoughts

ALL THROUGH THIS BOOK THE terms *anger, hostility, rage, aggravation, stress*, and *anxiety* have been used liberally, but without specific analysis. Obviously, all these terms are related. Again obviously, they each describe various levels of intensity of the same feeling. Perhaps, if we place these terms along a continuum and relate them to various health maladies, we can begin to see just how dangerous and destructive it is to hold anger and hostile emotions inside.

The Relationship of Anger to Health

	Elevated heart rate	physical tension	elevated blood pressure	shallow breathing	churning stomach, ulcers	racing heart,	heart attack, cancer	psychotic break
Stress	Elevated heart rate							
Tension	Elevated heart rate	physical tension						
Anxiety	Elevated heart rate	physical tension	elevated blood pressure					
Resentment	Elevated heart rate	physical tension	elevated blood pressure	shallow breathing				
Anger	Elevated heart rate	physical tension	elevated blood pressure	shallow breathing	churning stomach, ulcers			
Hostility	Elevated heart rate	physical tension	elevated blood pressure	shallow breathing	churning stomach, ulcers	racing heart,		
Aggression	Elevated heart rate	physical tension	elevated blood pressure	shallow breathing	churning stomach, ulcers	racing heart,	heart attack, cancer	
Fury	Elevated heart rate	physical tension	elevated blood pressure	shallow breathing	churning stomach, ulcers	racing heart,	heart attack, cancer	psychotic break

In the process of living, there are many opportunities for conflict. Some issues are truly beyond our control. However, the majority of situations we face—if we are willing—we *can* have an impact on. The important thing to remember is this: holding things inside is not healthy. We pay an intestinal price for holding on to our anger feelings. It is okay to be angry. The only question is: how do you want to deal with yours? You do have choices. You are in control.

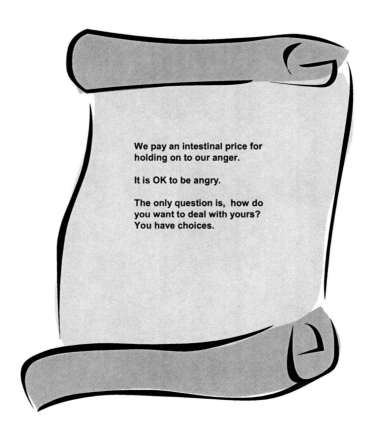

We pay an intestinal price for holding on to our anger.

It is OK to be angry.

The only question is, how do you want to deal with yours? You have choices.

Additional Resources

Assertive Communication

Bach, George and Herb Goldberg. *Creative Aggression: The Art of Assertive Living.* New York, NY: Doubleday, 1975.

Bach, George and Peter Wyden. *The Intimate Enemy: How to Fight Fair in Love and Marriage.* New York, NY: William Morrow, 1983.

Bower, Sharon and Gordon. *Asserting Yourself: A Practical Guide for Positive Change.* Reading, MA: Addison Wesley, 2004.

Elgin, Susan. *The Gentle Art of Verbal Self-Defense.* Inglewood, NJ: Prentice Hall, 2000.

Smith, Manuel. *When I Say No, I Feel Guilty.* New York, NY: Dial Press, 1985.

Conflict Management

Cloke, Kenneth and Joan Goldsmith. *Resolving Personal and Organizational Conflict.* San Francisco, CA: Jossey-Bass, 2000.

Deutsch, Morton; Peter Coleman, Editors. *The Handbook of Conflict Resolution.* San Francisco, CA: Jossey-Bass, 2000.

Wilmot, William and Joyce Hocker. *Interpersonal Conflict.* New York, NY: McGraw-Hill, 2007.

Body Language

Dimitrius, Jo-Ellan and Mark Mazzarella. *Reading People.* New York, NY: Random House, 2008.

Fast, Julius. *Body Language.* New York, NY: M. Evans and Company, 2002.

Nierenberg, Gerard and Henry Calero. *How to Read a Person Like a Book.* New York, NY: Hawthorn Books. 2009.

Negotiation Skills

Fisher, Roger and William Ury. *Getting To Yes.* Boston, MA: Houghton Mifflin, 2009.

Stark, Peter and Jane Flaherty. *The Only Negotiating Guide You'll Ever Need.* New York, NY: Broadway Books, 2003.

Nierenberg, Gerard and Henry Calero. *The New Art of Negotiating.* New York, NY: Hawthorn Books, 2009.

Right Brain-Left Brain Information

Buzan, Tony. *Use Both Sides of Your Brain; New Mind-Mapping Techniques.* New York, NY: E. P. Dutton & Company, 1991.

Wonder, Jacquelyn and Priscilla Donovan. *Whole-Brain Thinking.* New York, NY: William Morrow and Company, 1992.

Managing Anger and Hostility

Kassinove, Howard and Raymond Tafrate. *Anger Management.* Atascadero, CA: Impact Publishers, 2007.

Carter, Les and Frank Minirth. *The Anger Trap.* San Francisco, CA: Jossey-Bass, 2004.

Gentry, Doyle. *Anger-Free: Ten Basic Steps to Managing Your Anger.* New York, NY: Harper, 2000.

Potter-Efron, Ronald. *Rage. A Step-by-Step Guide to Overcoming Explosive Anger.* Oakland, CA: New Harbinger Publications, 2007.

Psychological Background

Beier, Ernst and Evans Valens. *People-Reading: How We Control Others, How They Control Us.* New York, NY: Stein & Day, 1981.
Goleman, Daniel. *Emotional Intelligence.* New York, NY: Bantam Books, 2006.
Seligman, Martin. *What You Can Change and What You Can't.* New York, NY: Alfred A. Knopf, 2007.